Praise for Minimalist Parenting
and Christine Koh and Asha Dornfest

"In *Minimalist Parenting*, Christine Koh and Asha Dornfest offer readers a much-welcome alternative to the usual parenting advice. With its focus on simplicity, self-knowledge, kindness, and confidence, this book gives parents the tools to help themselves—and, more importantly, trust themselves—as they navigate the often overwhelming terrain of managing family life."

—Andrea J. Buchanan, *New York Times* bestselling author of *The Daring Book for Girls*

"For any parents who feel overwhelmed with clutter in their homes, their schedules, or their brains (that is, just about every parent!), *Minimalist Parenting* is an invaluable guide to making family life more serene—and more fun."

—Gretchen Rubin, *New York Times* bestselling author of *Happier at Home* and *The Happiness Project*

"Who says that parenting has to be about buying, watching, fretting, obsessing and scheduling? Well, no one—in those words. But for many folks, that's what it is. Here's a way to say goodbye to the treadmill and howdy to happiness, extra space, and free time."

—Lenore Skenazy, author of *Free-Range Kids*

"Full of clear examples, helpful frameworks, and flat out wisdom from two sincere authors, *Minimalist Parenting* will help you identify exactly what your family needs are and how to fill those needs. Read this book and you'll give yourself permission to say no to the activities and habits that are putting a drag on your family, and yes to the options that build a satisfying life."

—Gabrielle Blair, author of *Design Mom* and founder of *Alt Summit*

"In *Minimalist Parenting* Koh and Dornfest offer keen insights about how to live a less stressful parenting life. This is a practical, comprehensive guidebook that also feels like a good, supportive, and upbeat friend. Harried parents may not have time to read it, which is exactly why they should."
—Katherine Ozment, contributing editor at *Boston* magazine

"A sensible, calming tonic for parents trying to escape the maelstrom of impossible social expectations and unbearable childrearing anxiety."
—Cory Doctorow, author of *Little Brother*

"What a great idea—for top parenting bloggers Christine Koh and Asha Dornfest to create a book, sharing their lessons learned and curating other advice from wise bloggers about how to simplify our lives as parents so we can enjoy everyday moments more. I was particularly inspired by the many unique suggestions about decluttering!"
—Ellen Galinsky, president of *Families and Work Institute* and author of *Mind in the Making*

"In parenting, less is turning out to be more. But how much less? And which less, exactly? *Minimalist Parenting* helps you figure it out in ways that fit your schedule, your style, and—most importantly—your values."
—Katherine Center, author of *The Bright Side of Disaster* and *Everyone Is Beautiful*

"Asha Dornfest and Christine Koh buck the trend toward 'expert' parenting by encouraging parents to trust in their own competence. *Minimalist Parenting* goes further, providing practical tips for managing time, stuff, and perspective."
—Chris Anderson, former editor-in-chief of *Wired Magazine* and founder of *GeekDad*

"When we exercise our creativity—and make something from nothing—we define ourselves. In this vivid and generous guide, Christine Koh and Asha Dornfest offer a practical and inspiring approach to creating the space for you and your family to thrive. You will be a happier person for having read this book."
—Emma Lively, co-author (with Julia Cameron) of *The Prosperous Heart* and *The Artist's Way for Parents*

"From the moment I read their phrase 'wrestling with abundance' I knew that Christine and Asha were on to something. *Minimalist Parenting* is just the boost you need. The tidbits of wisdom from some of my favorite bloggers on how they've handled the inevitable curveballs of parenting was inspiring reading for this newish mom."

—Jory Des Jardins, co-founder of BlogHer
and mother of two

"If you learn how to be a minimalist parent, you'll have a maximalist's amount of time to love your family and life. I trust Asha Dornfest and Christine Koh with this stuff. This book is a go-to resource!"

—Chris Brogan, CEO of *Human Business Works*
and author of *The Impact Equation*

"*Minimalist Parenting* is the solution to today's over-scheduled, over-stressed, and over-tired family. Filled to the brim with practical tips, tricks, and shortcuts, this guide to modern parenthood encourages parents to release the guilt and embrace a system that *works*. A must-read for every parent who finds herself struggling for air in a sea of parenting pressure."

—Erin Loechner, founder and editor of *Design For Mankind* and *Design For Minikind*

"The goal of *Minimalist Parenting* is stunningly simple—to keep the stuff that increases joy and reduce what doesn't. There aren't enough books like this in the parenting space! Reading it boosted my confidence."

—Heather Flett & Whitney Moss, publishers of
Rookie Moms and 510 Families and
authors of *Stuff Every Mom Should Know*
and *The Rookie Mom's Handbook*

"Wow. I wish this book had been around when I was still struggling with school, sports, music, meals, and the occasional meltdown! That said, there are lots of tips and much wisdom that is helpful to anyone trying to 'minimize' what it takes to get happily through the day. I will keep my copy ready at hand!"

—Ginny Wolfe, senior director of strategic
relationships, *The ONE Campaign*

"*Minimalist Parenting* is the must-have book for any mom who feels her life is spiraling out of control. To-do lists, obligations, and commitments no longer have to define your days, nights and weekends. Learn from Christine and Asha how to reduce the physical and mental clutter, prioritize what's most important, and define parenting on your own terms, once and for all!"
—Erin Kane and Kristin Brandt, co-hosts of
The Manic Mommies Podcast

"This book is filled with honest, practical, and useful advice that will help any parent keep their sanity. Thankfully not just another parenting book, but a strategic guide to keeping your family happy and on track."
—C.C. Chapman, author of *Amazing Things Will Happen* and founder of *Digital Dads*

"*Minimalist Parenting* is marvelous, rare, and generous thing: a parenting help resource that actually helps. Where others often overwhelm and oppress parents with "expert" advice, Asha and Christine provide affirmation, support, and invaluable counterweight to a frantic culture."
—Kyran Pittman, author of *Planting Dandelions, Field Notes from a Semi-Domesticated Life*

"In a culture of too much, *Minimalist Parenting* helps orient your compass to the important. Koh and Dornfest teach you to block out the background noise and focus on what matters most to you and your family. This book is like a warm embrace, helping you see that in fact everything will be alright."
—Isabel Kallman, founder of *Alpha Mom*

"Christine Koh and Asha Dornfest have masterfully shown a fast-paced generation that scaling back is not only doable, but extremely beneficial to any family's overall well-being and contentment."
—Jennifer James, founder of *Mom Bloggers Club* and *Mom Bloggers for Social*

"In this era when parents get constant signals to speed up, sign up, and schedule every waking minute, it's refreshing that someone is finally saying it's alright to slow down and reclaim those serendipitous moments with our kids. For helicopter parents who can't slow down, *Minimalist Parenting* offers a welcome landing pad."
—Dave Pell, author of *NextDraft – The Day's Most Fascinating News*

MINIMALIST
parenting

MINIMALIST

parenting

ENJOY MODERN FAMILY LIFE
MORE BY DOING LESS

CHRISTINE KOH
ASHA DORNFEST

bibliomotion
books + media

First published by Bibliomotion, Inc.

33 Manchester Road
Brookline, MA 02446
Tel: 617-934-2427
www.bibliomotion.com

Printed in the United States of America

Library of Congress Cataloging-in-Publication Data

Koh, Christine K., 1973-
  Minimalist parenting : enjoy modern family life more by doing
less / by Christine Koh & Asha Dornfest.
      pages cm
    ISBN 978-1-937134-34-1 (pbk. : alk. paper)—ISBN 978-1-937134-35-8
(ebook)—ISBN 978-1-937134-36-5 (enhanced ebook)
  1. Parenting.   2. Parenthood.   I. Dornfest, Asha.   II. Title.
  HQ755.8.K637 2013
  649'.1—dc23
                                            2012047155

Christine Koh: To Jon, Laurel, and Violet—every day with you is a gift for which I'm incredibly grateful.

Asha Dornfest: To my parents, Rosalyn and Jagdish Jirge, for teaching me about love and trust. To my family, Rael, Sam, and Mirabai, for opening my world and my heart.

Contents

Introduction

As you scan the panorama of your life, you ultimately know you have a lot for which to be grateful. You have a wonderful family, a comfortable home, and plenty of opportunity as you look toward the future. Life's not perfect and there may be some problems to work out, but overall, things are good.

So why do you have a nagging sense that something's not right? Family life feels so full it's ready to burst. The schedule is packed, the house is cluttered, and your mind lacks clarity. It feels as if the many wonderful things in your life are crowding out something important—but what?

You know many families struggle with less security and fewer opportunities. You look around and it seems everyone else is juggling family life well enough. Perhaps you feel a little foolish for even *thinking* you might have a problem. But try as you might, you find yourself plagued by worry that you're somehow not doing enough, and that if you slow down, you'll zap your kids' chances at...happiness? Success? Something. You're not sure what, but you're not going to risk it.

We've been there. We still go there sometimes. But we've discovered a way to navigate past the self-doubt, guilt, and overwhelm inherent in today's parenting climate to a place of clarity, connection, and—most of all—fun. We call it *Minimalist Parenting*.

What Is Minimalist Parenting?

Minimalist Parenting operates on the knowledge that *right now*, you have everything you need to live the family life you want. You have enough time to fully engage in parenting while still caring for yourself, your work, and your relationships. You have enough expertise, enough love, enough stuff, and enough confidence to give your kids a remarkable childhood and a running start on a happy adulthood.

The obstacle standing between you and a happier, less overwhelming version of your family life isn't something that you're doing wrong. It's that you're *wrestling with abundance*—too many choices, too many obligations, too much stuff, and too much guilt about trying to do it all.

It's no wonder. Never before have parents been faced with so many choices—of child-rearing philosophies, work schedules, educational options, savings plans, gadgets and gear, nutritional advice, even entertainment possibilities for our dwindling free time. The opportunity, comfort, and security of modern life inevitably come with decisions to make about each of these things, and many more.

Choice is good, but the sheer magnitude of choice we face today is overwhelming, even paralyzing. *Minimalist Parenting* is our prescription for how to handle too much of a good thing. We'll show you how to *minimalize* your family life—how to edit your schedule, possessions, and expectations so there's more of what you love and care about and less of what you don't.

Gradually, you and your family will be able to enjoy the freedom that comes with your newly found room to breathe. Imagine life as a minimalist parent:

- Your decisions come more easily because they're based on *your* values, not a fear of missing the boat or doing something wrong.
- Your schedule isn't packed to the gills with things you feel you *should* be doing. Instead, there's time to take care of your professional obligations and the requisite errands, homework, and appointments, and also jigsaw puzzles, bike rides, snowball fights, impromptu potlucks, occasional evenings out, and time to take care of yourself.
- Your home becomes a base for creative projects, raucous slumber parties, quiet evenings, warm memories, and plenty of open, free time instead of a repository for endless obligations and failed attempts at domestic perfection.
- You still enjoy buying things, but you choose your purchases

based on what will decrease your long-term stress and increase your long-term joy.

- Your kids have free time "padding" their activities and lessons, giving them the chance to explore, entertain themselves, and find out what excites and interests them.
- Feeding your family goes from the Gordian Knot of planning for and preparing a daily array of well balanced, beautifully presented meals to a simple and nourishing part of your weekly routine.
- You can relax and enjoy the magic of your kids growing up.

This isn't some Pollyanna fantasy of life over the rainbow. You can do this, and we're going to help you figure out how.

We don't profess to have Zen-like, perfect lives. If you spent a week at our houses, you'd see plenty of chaos and dust bunnies. But we *have* identified concrete steps that will help you reframe your thinking and craft a lifestyle so you can become a happier, more confident parent. It's time to redefine what it means to have it all. On your terms.

This book is as much about "life optimization" as it is about parenting. The prerequisite for a relaxed family life is the space in your schedule, home, and budget to be able to live it. Ironically enough, it takes work to create that space, and that's where we come in. We'll help you identify what matters and brings joy to your family, and we'll show you how to clear away the physical and mental clutter that's getting in the way. Our intention isn't to tell you how to parent, it's to show you how to find your *own* parenting "right."

It's worth clarifying that our interpretation of minimalism veers from the traditional definition. Minimalist Parenting is not about living like a Spartan or a monk (we love our vacations and brownies too much for that). You don't need to become tightfisted or anti-achievement or saintly. There are no rigid rules to follow because each family's path is unique.

At the heart of Minimalist Parenting is formal permission to step off the modern parenting treadmill, and to have fun while you're doing it. You're not blowing your children's shot at success—just the opposite. Living a joyous life that's in line with your values (instead of some manufactured version of "successful" modern parenthood) will give your kids room to grow into the strong, unique people they are meant to be. More importantly, this way of being will provide a model that shows your kids how to trust their instincts as they move toward inde-pendence and adulthood. Finally, Minimalist Parenting will allow you to claim space in your own wonderful life. This is your journey as much as it is theirs.

As you embrace Minimalist Parenting, the roller coaster of family life goes from anxiety provoking to fun. You'll still experience the white-knuckle drops, the ups and downs, and a few blind turns. But you'll be strapped in with direction and confidence, and *you'll enjoy the crazy ride.*

Who We Are

What do we know about Minimalist Parenting? We're both busy par-ents: between us we're juggling four kids, two husbands, several blogs, businesses and jobs, writing and social media careers, thousands of e-mails, business travel, two urban homes, and a dog. We know all about getting buried by what seems at first to be a good problem to have—lives full of opportunity in this fast-paced world that thrives on "more."

Christine Koh

I'm the sixth of seven children—I grew up in a multigenerational house-hold where my immigrant parents worked incredibly hard to keep both our nuclear family and various relatives afloat. At any given time, there were a dozen people, give or take, filling every nook and cranny of our three-bedroom home.

The affluent, predominantly Caucasian Boston suburb of my youth was a challenging environment in which to be so plainly different—both racially and socioeconomically. The racial slurs were painful, yes, but per-haps even more difficult to cope with was my embarrassment when kids in my class pointed out that I had worn the same shirt three days in a row (which was due as much to my lack of an expansive wardrobe as the fact that I really, really liked that shirt) or when I was excluded from the cafeteria table because I did not meet the minimum sitting requirement of owning three pairs of Guess jeans and two Benetton insignia sweaters.

These social hardships were challenging, as were dynamics at home, but there was also a lot of love. My father was tough (even terrifying at times) but had a soft, charming side that I fully discovered later in life. My mother was the rock—she held everything together despite immense and sometimes intense challenges. And though it wasn't puppy dogs and unicorns all the time, my siblings and I share a deep sense of solidarity given everything we endured together.

Since becoming a parent, I have had many moments of internal conflict—stuck between the practical values instilled in me by my parents and the potential to overcompensate because of a childhood replete with exclusion. Ultimately, after much experimentation—and the irony of finding myself in a career where I now experience abundance—I learned that it *was* possible to find a middle ground. That I could acquire things I loved or found beautiful or interesting or meaningful without going over the cliff to excess. That there were ways for my children to experience cool things without becoming spoiled and entitled. That it was possible for me to find my own way, and to not only be okay *not* being the Tiger Mom, but also to appreciate that other parents—Tiger or otherwise—are ultimately working through their own issues and stumbling along trying to find their way, just as I am. That we're all in this together, doing the best we can for our kids and ourselves in each moment.

Childhood issues aside, why did I feel compelled and qualified to write this book with Asha? First, I have always been a writer and a sharer. As a child, I wrote stories. In high school and college, I was a reporter and editor of the school newspapers. In my previous professional life I was an academic: I completed a BA with a double major in music and psychology at Wheaton College, a master's degree in cognitive psychology at Brandeis University, a PhD in brain, behavior, and cognitive science with a focus on music and pedagogy at Queen's University in Ontario, Canada, and a three-year postdoctoral fellowship with joint appointments at MIT, Massachusetts General Hospital, and Harvard Medical School. I have written scholarly articles and have a rather meaty dissertation gathering dust in my basement. Since leaving academia for the freelance world, I have written thousands of blog posts and articles in the lifestyle and parenting space.

Second, every day I live the demands of negotiating a career and parenthood. As an academic I worked long hours in the lab while trying to juggle motherhood (pumping breast milk while squatting on the floor of a single-stall bathroom at MIT was a particular low) and wrestled with the guilt of sending Laurel to day care (those days I would only see her a few hours a day, tops, before and after school) and the limited time in which to take care of everything not related to my job or my baby. I now have a "flexible" career (notice the use of quotes) in the sense that I work out of my home office. However, I work as many or more hours than I did as an academic, given my creative palette, which includes my work as founder/editor of the parenting/lifestyle blog *Boston Mamas*, founder/designer at Posh Peacock (graphic design firm), consultant at Women Online (digital strategy firm), cofounder of The Mission List (social media for social good community/consultancy) and Pivot Boston (event series for making your life awesome), managing editor of the academic journal *Music Perception*, not to mention my other freelance writing and advisory commitments, writing this book, and regular travel for work. The key difference between my previous and current professional lives is that I became miserable in academia and love what I do now.

Also, I now have two children: Violet attends day care part-time and Laurel is in public school but is reluctant to participate in camps and after-school programs. What this means time-wise is that I don't have full-time covered working hours during the day, work many nights, and have taken an impressive number of conference calls while nursing a baby, stretching, or eating my lunch. And I still have other professional dreams: future books, magazine writing, and on-camera work.

Third, like you, aside from my identity as parent, I'm a cog in a system of relationships. I married Jon in 2000; he is my favorite human on the planet and is, by virtue of being the person closest to me, sometimes at risk for getting what we (only sort of jokingly) refer to as "the dregs of Christine Koh." I also am a daughter, an in-law, a sister, an aunt, a cousin, a niece, a friend, and a community member—with all of the associated get-togethers, requests, correspondence, and periodic crises that contribute to a full and sometimes complicated life.

All of this is to say that *I get it*. Every single day I live the awesomeness and the challenges of being a parent and a professional. I have my share of freak-outs. However, the reason I have felt so compelled to write this book (which has been percolating in my brain since 2010) is that I've been on a quest over the last several years to—forgive my bluntness—cut the crap. To focus on what's important and to minimalize the obligations and "angry brownies" (keep reading because you'll benefit from the angry brownie story) and toxic people (yes, it's been crucial to minimalize toxic people) in my life so my bandwidth is less cluttered. So there's more "happy and awesome Christine Koh" and less "dregs of Christine Koh." Every day brings its challenges and the journey is an evolving one, but I've made a hell of a lot of progress. I know how palpable the pain points are for so many parents and I want to help people out of that woeful, aching, and stuck place. I hope you'll stick with Asha and me for this ride from dregs to awesome. We applaud you for showing up.

Asha Dornfest

My upbringing was solidly middle-class and happily uncomplicated. I'm the only child of an Indian father and a Jewish mother of Eastern European decent, and my childhood was distinctly centered in American Suburbia.

Growing up, there was no sibling conflict, no difficulty in school, and no questions about where I fit into the world. We lived a modest life but there were no major wants. Struggle wasn't something I was familiar with. My relatively easy, happy life continued all the way through college, marriage to my husband, Rael, and the beginning of my career as a writer.

While I was still happy, becoming a mother marked the end of easy. My day-to-day routine and self-image changed so dramatically that happiness was no longer my effortless, default state of being. It now took work I had no experience doing.

As my kids grew and changed, I embarked on a crooked journey toward a family life that worked for all of us. I struggled to find solutions in books and the experiences of seemingly knowing older parents, but always came up short. What worked for other families just didn't seem to work for mine... or for me. For a time I thought it was a failure of my own parenting (those were long, hard years), but I slowly came to realize that parenting is more about being open to learning than it is about knowing the answer.

In 2005, I started a blog called *Parent Hacks* as a way to talk with other parents and swap ideas and discoveries about parenting. Those were the days before Facebook and Twitter, so the community that grew at *Parent Hacks* felt somewhat magical to me. So many other parents were stumbling along as I was, trying to follow their own paths to a balanced family life, and we could all talk about it and help each other along. We began a fascinating conversation that continues there today.

As *Parent Hacks* grew, so did the complexity of parenting. The early school years proved to be extremely difficult for my oldest child, Sam. As a grade-schooler he suffered from anxiety, and the resulting fallout at school was disastrous to his health and self-esteem. Thus began our family's three-year odyssey through the school and medical systems. It was a frightening and stressful time, especially because it coincided with my husband's founding of an Internet start-up. My daughter, Mirabai, was thriving in school, but Sam continued to struggle. Anxiety had effectively halted Sam's learning, and we were out of options. In the middle of Sam's fourth-grade year, we made a decision to do something I said I would never do: we decided to homeschool him.

I could write an entire book about what I learned during the maddening, delightful, eye-opening year and a half we spent educating Sam at home (and perhaps I will someday!). But for the purposes of *Minimalist Parenting*, my two biggest takeaways were confidence in my parenting decisions and trust in my kids. Many people disagreed with our choice to take Sam out of school, including people whose opinion and approval I valued. But we knew it was the right thing to do, even though we had no idea what was in store for us (and, frankly, we were petrified).

Eventually I found that the more I paid attention to my values and my family's unique needs—and the less I was distracted by parenting experts, social pressures, and the opinions of well-meaning peers—the easier and better our family life became.

Today, both Sam and Mirabai are doing wonderfully at their local schools, and Sam's anxiety is a thing of the past. My family is no longer in the grip of fearing for our child's health. My husband and I are both doing work we love while watching our two amazing (and very different) kids grow up. And I believe, with all my heart, that Minimalist Parenting (even though I didn't call it that at the time) is what helped us get here. We've still got a ways to go, and we still wrestle with balance and all the other complications of modern life. But we're happy, we're healthy, and we're learning.

What You'll Find in This Book

Minimalist Parenting is as much a mind-set as it is a set of recommendations for simplifying and streamlining your family life. In order to minimalize your life in ways that are *lasting*, we'll guide you to shift your perspective as well as your practice.

We focus on the early to middle years of parenting (newborn to about age twelve) because those years place the biggest constraints on your time and space. We also see Minimalist Parenting as a way to build toward strong, healthy teen years. By the time kids are teenagers, the parenting focus shifts from direct care and teaching to promoting their independence, guiding and supporting their exploration, and preparing them for launch into adulthood. They'll be making their own choices and navigating the path to self-reliance, hopefully with a well-internalized dose of your minimalist modeling on board.

We lay the foundational groundwork for Minimalist Parenting in chapter 1. In it, we explain the six simple—but key—assumptions underlying Minimalist Parenting.

The next five chapters will help you clear the path to a calmer family life by minimalizing its major "containers." Chapters 2 and 3 help you manage and open up your (and your family's) schedule. Chapters 4 and 5 address the whys and hows of clearing your space and decluttering your stuff. Chapter 6 offers our minimalist approach to money and spending, with tips for simplifying your financial setup.

The next six chapters move on to minimalizing day-to-day family life with children. Chapter 7 is all about rethinking playtime, and how fun and friendship don't require a house brimming with toys. Chapters 8 and 9 offer our minimalist approach to the school years (while inviting you to *enlarge* your definition of education). We devote chapter 10 to extracurricular activities, providing suggestions for how to balance your kids' interests and learning opportunities with open, unstructured time for the entire family. In chapters 11 and 12, you'll find out how to minimalize mealtime: planning your menus so you're no longer caught unprepared, and "rightsizing" your expectations about family meals.

Chapter 13 addresses the special occasions in our lives. We focus on ways to keep the fun and joy of celebrations, holidays, and travel while losing the stress and excess.

Finally, we wrap up right where we started: with you. We devote chapter 14 to self-care: why you need it, how to embrace it, and, now that you have the space in your life, what you might like to do.

Throughout the book, you'll find anecdotes and contributions that help bring our concepts to life, whether from us (called out by our avatars), other parents (called out by a conversation bubble), or fellow colleagues in the parenting/lifestyle writing space (laid out as sidebars).

Minimalist Parenting is just the beginning. In the resources section, we share some of our favorite books, websites, apps, and other tools that will help you continue your journey to a happier, less cluttered life.

You'll find even more inspiration on the *Minimalist Parenting* website (minimalistparenting.com). Printable worksheets, activities and a community of support awaits you when you're ready to move beyond the book.

Buckle up: it's going to be an exciting ride. The scenery is fantastic and you're headed somewhere remarkable. Let's go.

1

The Road to Minimalist Parenting

Y ou've just taken off on a road trip with your two new best friends, Fewer and Less. The six key ideas in this chapter are the compass points on your road map. Actually, *treasure map* is a better metaphor, because there's no specific route you're expected to take to get to the payoff. This journey will be more like navigating by the stars and the landmarks—with frequent stops to enjoy the view.

The first step toward Minimalist Parenting is to embrace a new mind-set that challenges the modern parenting prescription of "more." As you reframe your unique constraints and assumptions, you'll begin to understand how your life, once minimalized, can take on a shape you envision and create. What follows are the attitude shifts and perspective changes that will help you pull it off.

Make Room for Remarkable

If we're talking about compass points, this one is true north. When you get rid of the stuff you don't love, there's more room for the stuff you do love. A simple statement on the face of it, but incredibly powerful when applied to your life.

A million things want your attention. The birthday gifts that need buying, the plans that need making, the after-school programs that need arranging, just to name a few. One of the benefits of modern parenting is the sheer amount of choice available in just about every aspect of family life.

But the more choices, decisions, and stuff you must wade through, the more remote your remarkable life becomes. Have you ever spent fifteen minutes at the drugstore staring at the array of cold medicines, wondering which will best help your feverish, bedridden kid? Which is the *right* one? Fifteen minutes may not sound like much, but when you add up all the time and attention lost managing the barrage of choices thrown at you each day, each month…it adds up fast. More than that, the mental clutter that results casts a shadow over everything.

As one who tends toward over-research, it has taken me a long time to let go of my need to investigate everything. I've learned to shorten my search for the "best" answer and to just go with what's most likely to do the job. The time and mental space I've freed up feels like oxygen for my brain.

Minimalist Parenting is about editing. Your time and attention are too precious to be nibbled away by everything that would thoughtlessly take a bite. You're panning for gold, swirling your life around to reveal the gleaming nuggets and letting the silt and debris wash away. When you edit out the unnecessary—whether these are physical items, activities, expectations, or maybe even a few people—you make room for remarkable.

The goal is actually quite simple: keep or add the stuff that increases the joy, meaning, and connection in your life, and reduce or get rid of the stuff that doesn't.

It's not exactly revolutionary to suggest that reducing clutter in one's life increases one's happiness. But unlike decluttering your house, decluttering your life can be a lot murkier. How do you know which things to keep and which to toss?

Know Yourself

When we encourage you to focus on joy, we're not talking about a flash of momentary happiness. We're talking about living in alignment with your deeply held values. When you make decisions based on your values (as opposed to what all the external voices in your life are telling you to do), something inside goes *zing*. Not always immediately, and not always obviously, but it zings nonetheless.

Therefore, to figure out how to edit your life, you must first identify your unique set of values. "Values" is a lofty word—begging for Capitalization Due To Importance—but in reality your values are probably pretty humble and approachable. Simply stated: your values are the things you believe deep down.

Some of your values come straight from your upbringing (for better or worse). We all come from somewhere, and accepting that a big chunk of ourselves is bound up in our family culture is an important part of becoming a grown-up. For example, perhaps you—like us—have frugal tendencies instilled in you by the cultures of your parents. Or perhaps your glamorous mother passed on her exquisite taste in fashion and design. Or maybe you grew up playing in the woods, so you consider time outdoors to be a priority for your kids.

Other values may be in direct opposition to those of your family of origin. If yours was a cold, formal household, you may consider emotional warmth and laughter to be cornerstones of your parenting. If your parents withheld treats, you may believe in your kids' right to a bucket full of Halloween candy.

The good news is you can cherry-pick the best of what you grew up with. (It may take some therapy to get there, but you can do it.) Take some time to zero in on your unique values. Everyone's values are different so there are no wrong answers. No one will judge you on saintliness or profundity. Ask yourself:

- What am I grateful my parents taught me?
- What do I want to do differently from my parents?
- What do I want my family to represent?
- What do I care about? (If it's easier to use the process of elimination, then ask, What *don't* I care about?)
- What do I want my kids to take with them as they go out into the world?
- What roles do I want to play—as a spouse/partner, professional, and/or part of whatever village or community I've created for my family?

Zeroing in on your values is an ongoing process, so don't worry if your answers feel incomplete. Keep a notebook handy and scribble down relevant insights as they pop up. The most important thing you can do now is begin the excavation process. As you reveal the edges of your values, keep chiseling away and the bigger picture will emerge over time.

Know Your Family

While you're considering your values, it's important to recognize that your family members come with their own unique blueprints and a spirit and a constitution that may be different from yours. What if you and your partner crave adventure and excitement, but your kid is a homebody? You may feel at home surrounded by your books, but your partner is constantly trying to get you to go to social events. One kid may happily accompany you on errands while the other requires more control over his daily routine. (That's the one screaming in the airplane seat behind you.)

 I wouldn't call my husband, Rael, and I opposites, because we hold so many basic values in common. But our day-to-day styles—how we operate in our daily lives—are very different. I'm fundamentally social, preferring to do things in a group or a community. He draws energy from quiet time at home and alone. I'm an intuitive decision maker who resists holding myself to a tight structure, which means my homemaking skills are ... still emerging. He finds peace in routine and proceeds through his day systematically (and his office is spotless).

We've had to work on accepting each other's innate styles and on finding common ground so that we could create a unified family culture and consistently parent our kids. At the same time, we try to acknowledge each other's individual strengths and quirks ... they attracted us to each other in the first place. It's a long-term process we revisit constantly as circumstances, goals, kids (and we) change.

Consider the following questions about each person in your family:

- If I were to describe my partner/kid using a single word, what would it be?
- In what ways are we similar?
- In what ways are we really, really different?
- My partner/kid is happiest when s/he is _____.
- What activities does s/he most enjoy?

We're not suggesting you throw your dreams in the trash because of differences in family temperament. The key is to navigate toward a life that allows family members space and permission to be themselves while providing opportunities to stretch and learn something new. After all, even homebodies (especially homebodies, perhaps) need encouragement and opportunity to step over the threshold into the big, exciting world.

You're bound to run into roadblocks, especially in families with several different temperaments. Remember, too, you're still getting to know your kids, especially if they're young. Plus, they're constantly changing and so are you—so even your best answers are educated guesses and may be completely off base six months from now. That's okay. Just note your discoveries (the notebook!) and keep them in mind as you proceed.

Trust Your Decisions

You're getting in touch with what makes you and your family members tick…go you! You're driving the bus, and now it's time to give that internal voice of yours—the one that quietly knows the way—the steering wheel.

Meet Your Inner Bus Driver

Your inner bus driver is your gut feeling, your internal sense of what's right and wrong. We each have an inner bus driver, but we don't always listen to or trust her. Sometimes we're so distracted by the noise and pressure around us, we can't even hear our inner bus drivers.

No longer. Your inner bus driver knows which way to go. All you need to do is listen. What (or whom) might you want to steer around? All the voices that keep telling you your opinions don't count. Parenting experts, lifestyle gurus, and marketers. Well-meaning relatives. Glossy magazine spreads. Outdated messages from your childhood. Your insecurities about the seemingly "put together" parents of your kids' friends. The narrow definitions of "right" inherent in the culture of modern parenting.

It's also time to embrace the role you and your partner play as leaders of your family. Today's parenting culture leans heavily toward recognizing each child's individuality and adjusting accordingly. In our hearts we believe this is a good thing, but parents must lead the way, guiding behavior and setting limits in the process.

So plunge a flag into the ground, stand tall, and claim this life as yours! It's not always easy to trust yourself when you feel utterly bewildered and the external voices sound so sure of themselves. It's even harder to resist comparing yourself to other parents who seem to have it all figured out, especially when your kid is screaming in the middle of the cereal aisle. But you know yourself and your kids even if it doesn't always feel like it, and it's your life to live. You owe it to yourself and your family to give your inner bus driver as much authority as the cacophony of voices around you. That bus driver knows more than you think.

Optimize Your "Information Comfort Zone"

We all have different ways we process options and make decisions. As you learn to trust your inner bus driver, identify your "information comfort zone"—the way you prefer to absorb and act on information—and tweak it to free up time and mental clarity and to reduce the mind-sucking tendency to dither. The following are some common decision-making styles and strategies for minimalizing each.

You Engage in Extensive Research

When faced with a decision or purchase, do you research every option available even though you can identify one or two promising choices pretty quickly?

(Warning: former Type-A confession ahead.) When I was deciding on baby gear for my first child, Laurel, I wanted to find the absolute best (read: perfect) option for each purchase. For example, when it was time to buy a crib, I read *Consumer Reports* reviews, visited local stores to peruse the options and poll the staff for their opinions, scoured multiple reviews online, and read baby gear review blogs. I tracked my findings in a spreadsheet and did a thorough analysis of pros and cons before making a decision. Despite my exhaustive research, with each purchase, I was continually nagged by the fact that there was always at least one thing that wasn't perfect.

The crux of the scenario lies in the last sentence: *there was always at least one thing that wasn't perfect.* If you're a researcher, you'll save a lot of time and energy by stopping the search at, say, three items with positive reviews from reliable sources. It's natural to want "only the best" for your child—simply broaden your definition from a binary best/not best choice to "one of several good options."

Another approach is to simply choose the shopping method that's most fun and stick to whatever choices are available. Voltaire hit the nail on the head: *Do not let the perfect be the enemy of the good.*

You Defer to Professional Authority

No one wants to be *that parent* who speed dials the pediatrician at the first sign of a cold. But no matter how much advice one gets from books, the Internet, or friends, some people just feel more comfortable talking to the doctor.

If that describes you, there's no need to feel embarrassed. One of the keys of Minimalist Parenting is to *know yourself*, which means starting at your own baseline without judgment. We'll always encourage you to have faith in your inner bus driver, but if it helps speed a decision, save yourself the stress and consult with an expert sooner rather than later. It's not a sign of defeat if you don't know what's going on or if you feel better making decisions as part of a team. Just remember: *you* hold the steering wheel. You're driving the bus.

You Feel Most Comfortable Following the Crowd

We've heard more than one parent compare the decision-making process around purchases and activities to high school. Peer pressure and insecurity often come into play, even when it's unintentional. If you're feeling unsure about your choices, it's natural to look around you to see what everyone else is doing. The problem is that everyone else isn't living your life or raising your kid.

Talk to friends about how they're handling various parenting choices and challenges, but then pause, check in with your inner bus driver, then make the decision that feels right for *your* family based on *your* values and *your* family's collective temperament.

Course Correction Beats Perfection

With the stakes so high (these *are* your children we're talking about), there's never been more pressure to be sure you're making the right choices. About *everything*. What if you make the wrong choice? Will you doom your kid to a life of mediocrity, or, at the very least, years of therapy?

First, we'd like to suggest that if you're reading this book in the first place you've already built a foundation based on good choices. You're loving and conscientious and are doing the best you can for your kid. Your child has the enormous gifts of love, education, and basic needs covered. Certainly, not every day is perfect, but the best intentions are there—which go a long way toward helping the pieces fall into place, even when you can't predict or control each one.

Second, not only does each decision you make lead to an array of possible outcomes—all of which add experience and color to your life—most of the time, you get do-overs. You don't need to worry about being "right" every time because you can change course. And who knows? As you recalculate the route to your destination, you may happen across an even more amazing adventure.

Pulling our son out of school was the scariest decision of our lives—not only had we never considered homeschooling, we had no idea how we would proceed.

But we gradually discovered that it wasn't all-or-nothing. At first, we felt like we had made an irreversible decision to jump off the grid and abandon "normal life," but in actuality we had just chosen to take a particular fork in the road. We could always make a change later on.

When I was pregnant with Laurel, I was an academic who identified as a researcher, and that identity translated to my parenting. I read and researched everything. I also was admittedly a little rigid when it came to toys and shunned all things battery-operated. Many things changed in the six-and-a-half years between Laurel and Violet—the most important being I listened to my instinct over "shoulds" and data when making personal and professional decisions. Every time I followed my instinct, it paid off. Every time I didn't, I got burned.

So while I was pregnant with Violet, other than taking good care of myself and following my midwife's instructions, I didn't read anything pregnancy-related. When my girlfriend Heidi offered to throw me a baby shower, I said yes, as long as we could make it a secondhand shower (which I describe further in chapter 4). It was so refreshing to get a do-over and enjoy approaching my second pregnancy *in the way that felt right to me.*

It's worth mentioning that among the piles of hand-me-downs I received when Violet arrived were battery-operated toys. Yes, some of them were too loud (a piece of duct tape over the speaker solved that problem), but this time around I didn't cling to my rigid parameters. And you know what? Violet couldn't be happier rocking out to those battery-operated musical toys.

It's important to acknowledge that, as we make choices, there are bound to be hard times and disappointments. Some will be the result of our decisions and others will be beyond our control. Our natural tendency as parents is to want to protect our kids from pain at all costs, but the truth is that each difficult experience has a lesson to teach, possibly even a gift to impart.

It's not wishy-washy to adjust your parenting approach as you and your kids grow. It shows that you're open to the bigness of the world and the changing needs of your family. You're humble and brave enough to learn as you go.

As you reduce the total number of decisions and choices in your life, try to dial down the intensity on the ones that remain. Each time you're faced with a choice, briefly investigate your options, check in with your inner bus driver to figure out which option feels most right (few options are *all* right), then go for it. You can always make adjustments as your ideas, kids, and circumstances change.

We're in This Together

Many parents operate under the illusion that "more" equals "safer" when it comes to their kids' future security. With all the pressure to give our kids a leg up on a successful adulthood, it's easy to lose sight of the important fact that *we're all on the same team.*

Part of the modern tendency toward overparenting seems to be driven by a fear of scarcity, whether it relates to material goods or spots at day care or enrollment in the "best" school. We don't buy it. We believe there's enough to go around. Sure, there's only one valedictorian and one first-chair violin. But the idea that your child's future success hinges on such a detail is an illusion.

We love our children so desperately that it's too frightening to accept that their futures are, in part, a result of circumstance. Their best chance for a happy adulthood lies in discovering and nurturing their strengths, cultivating flexibility in the face of obstacles, and developing the tools to forge lasting relationships. Following a minimalized, less cluttered path is the most direct route there.

You can choose to do less. *You* can choose to be present. And that's incredibly exciting. You can make things happen *now*. With your newly minimalized mind-set in place, you're ready to minimalize the rest of your life!

2

It's Your Time: Tuning In and Prioritizing

S how us a parent with enough time, and we'll show you some lovely waterfront property in the Arctic. Even now, we marvel that we've got the same number of hours we've always had. It seems like there's so much more to cram into every day.

Managing a family schedule is exponentially more complicated than handling your own. Not only is there simply *more* to fit into the calendar, the pressure is relentless to say yes to everything and do it all perfectly. If we listened to every parenting message coming at us, we'd think *every choice* is vitally important. Many of us operate under a perpetual measure of fear that if we don't sign our kids up for the camps or schedule the lessons or plan out a week's worth of home-cooked dinners, all while exercising, keeping a semi-decent home, managing a career, and maintaining more than a working relationship with our partner...we're somehow failing. In short, there are ever more ways to slice and dice your time and attention, and endless ways to feel bad about it.

We're not going to reveal the secret of doing it all. Because *no one* can do it all, no matter what the magazines and productivity blogs would have you think. Celebrity moms aren't doing it all, the well-groomed PTA member floating down the school hallway isn't doing it all, and your mom didn't do it all. But everyone can do *less* and still raise healthy, happy, intelligent, and responsible kids.

The key lies in fine-tuning your filters so only the important stuff makes it onto your worthy-of-attention radar. The question goes from "How do I fit everything in?" to "What's most important to fit in?" The beauty of this approach: when you minimalize your schedule, you have a shot at ending most days with the knowledge that you did most of the things that matter.

In this chapter, we'll take you through big-picture exercises that will give you a clearer sense of your family's priorities with regard to time and help you assess the way you currently spend time in light of those priorities. Then, we'll provide some strategies to help you close the gap between what you're doing and what you think is important to do.

Go grab your notebook and a pencil and let's get started.

Know Yourself

Before you can decide what's worthy of a calendar slot, you need to figure out your unique relationship with time. Understanding and honoring that relationship is the first step toward getting a grip on your schedule.

Recognize Your "Time Style"

It's safe to say we could all benefit from a tune-up of our time management skills. But to know where to begin, you need to identify your unique "time style." Your time style is the way in which you feel most comfortable managing and spending your time.

Let's take a step into fantasyland for a moment. If you were the only person in the picture, how would you spend your time? Answer the following questions (for now, don't worry about what seems realistic):

- Are you someone who likes to work from a schedule? Or do you prefer flexibility and spontaneity?
- Do you find comfort in predictable routines or do you feel hemmed in?

- Would your friends describe you as punctual? Would you? Do you care?
- Can you jump between activities easily, or do you need "breathing room" in between?
- If you had an ideal day off, would you plan an itinerary full of fabulous or would you discover your fun on the fly?
- Do you prefer spending time with people or alone? In what proportions?

Your answers will shed light on your ideal schedule based on planned-ness, filled-ness, and peopled-ness. For example, one person's ideal schedule might include a weekly errand day, regular chores and activities for the kids, and monthly potlucks. Another's might have few weekend plans (but plenty of possible options). There are endless ways to organize your time.

Play around with your answers to help solidify a vision of your ideal schedule, even if it seems impossible based on your work, commitments, or family life. Have fun with this! The goal is to get a clear picture of what you want before you map out the steps to get there.

Identify Your Golden Hours

Recognizing your time style is an important step toward building your family's schedule. The next step is to tune in to your body's natural rhythm. We've all got daily ups and downs of energy, and they're relatively predictable. To make the most of your schedule, identify the patterns so, as much as possible, you can do the brain-stretching work during the ups and save the mundane chores for the downs. Consider:

- When you need more time to yourself, do you prefer to get up early or stay up late?
- When do you feel most vital and energetic each day?
- Conversely, when do you experience major energy lows?

Again, you're still fantasizing here. Try to answer these questions based on *you*, not based on what seems doable or reasonable. If your energy level peaks from 3 to 5 p.m., but that's also when everyone's cranky after waking up from their naps, those are still golden hours. We'll deal with reality next.

Find Your Goldilocks Level of "Busy"

It's so easy for weeks to fly by and for commitments to stack up, and suddenly you're overwhelmed. Believe us, we've been there. Sometimes it's unavoidable and you just have to put your head down and barrel through. But often, that overwhelmed feeling is a function of unintentionally packing the schedule more tightly than your family can handle.

Try this experiment: look back on your calendar from the last month. For each week, look at how many commitments you and your kids had—count them up and jot down the number in your notebook. Now channel Goldilocks. Note the weeks that felt like too little was going on, the weeks that felt too full, and the weeks that felt just right.

What's your family's "just right" number of weekly commitments? Write this number (BIG) in your notebook. Later, when you're actually working with your calendar, you're going to shoot for that number of weekly commitments (or fewer, as last-minute engagements and illnesses invariably crop up).

Do a Time Inventory

Now that you're closing in on how you'd like your ideal schedule to look, let's examine how you're actually spending your time. But before we proceed, let's be crystal clear: no one will wag any disapproving fingers at you. We're not judging how you spend your time. We don't care if you spend three hours a day on Facebook, nine hours a day in an office, or ten hours per week watching reality TV. We're not assessing your level of school volunteerism, how much time you spend on housework, or whether or not you're a workaholic. A time inventory is simply a way for you to gather data about the current state of things so you can make mindful choices about spending your time. Here we go:

1. Take a few minutes to fill in the following grid. The categories are intentionally broad, and we left a few spaces empty so you can fill in your own. You can get more detailed if you like, but really, all you need is a big-picture look at how you're spending time during a typical day. Estimate how much time you spend on the following activities:

Activity	Hours per day	How it feels
Sleep		
Grooming/personal care		
Paid work, or your schoolwork/education		
Exercise		
Domestic chores (cleaning, bills, etc.)		
Errands (grocery shopping, going to the vet, etc.)		
Cooking		
Volunteer and/or community work		
Kid activities (playing, driving, diaper-changing, homework help, etc.)		
Family activities (mealtimes, sports, religious observance, etc.)		
Hobbies and recreation (yours, not everyone else's)		
Zone-out time (TV, web surfing, social media, etc.)		
Social activities (time with extended family and friends)		
Relationship-building (date night, chats with your partner, sex, etc.)		

Given that few parents' days are typical, you might want to track time estimates for a week or so, just to get a clearer picture of how you're spending your time. Do the numbers surprise you?

2. Now, jot down one or two words that describe your feelings about each category. Quick! Whatever comes to mind! No one is going to read this except for you—unless you want to share it—so try not to let shame or embarrassment get in the way. Remember: you're doing the best you can right now, and you're working through these exercises in an effort to make a change for the better. THIS IS YOU BEING BRAVE.

3. Now, time to evaluate: Does anything jump out at you as seeming out of whack? Does anything make you feel especially proud or cringe-y? Does the time you spend zoning out actually feel relaxing or like the scheduling equivalent of junk food—initially pleasurable but ultimately draining? What is your inner bus driver telling you? Write that down, too. That's important wisdom you'll use for the next activity.

Know Your Family's "Time Sense"

Now that you've spent some time evaluating your use of time, answer the following questions as best you can for each member of your family. Try not to place a value on the answers, even if they lead to behaviors that drive you nuts:

- Does your kid prefer being busy with plans and friends or spending "open" time alone or with you?
- Does your child naturally gravitate toward parceling out his time, or does he have little sense of or interest in how much time is passing?
- How does your child do with transitions from one activity to the next?
- Does your child naturally wake up early in the morning? Does she take naps during the day? What time is her ideal bedtime (for her, not necessarily for you)?
- What is your child's temperament? Is he strong-willed and independent? Easy-going? Compliant? Adventurous? Shy? Curious? Serious? Competitive? Silly?

If your child is still too young to give you many clues, just use these questions as a lens through which to think about your child's reactions to past experiences.

What about your partner? How does his or her approach to time mirror or differ from yours?

There are rarely black and white answers, which is fine. The idea here is to get a more complete picture of the way your family prefers to operate in the world…not unlike the exercise you did when you envisioned your own fantasy schedule.

Now, compare what you've written about your family's relationship with time and your own. Where is there overlap? Perhaps you and your kid are both early risers, so shared morning activities and errands are a possibility while your partner sleeps in. Where is there conflict? Maybe you hate too many restrictive plans but your kid (or partner) craves predictability. Make a note of overlaps and conflicts, as this will be crucial information for the next activity.

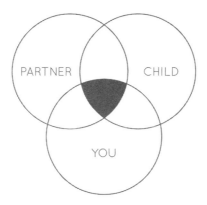

Make a More and Less List

You know where you want to end up (as close to your fantasy schedule as possible). You know where you are (your time inventory shed light on your current schedule, you have a sense of your "just right" number of weekly commitments, and you've given thought to your kids' relationship with time and how it might differ from yours). Now begins the task of deciding what to add to your schedule and what to cut.

Your tool: The More and Less List. It's just what it sounds like: a list of what you'd like more of in your life, as well as what you'd like less of.

Don't be fooled if a More and Less List sounds overly simple (perhaps even simplistic). It's a surprisingly powerful way to turn ideas into action. It's the beginning of the road map that leads from where you are to where you want to be. With a More and Less list, you're drawing in the big landmarks. As time goes on, you'll fill in the freeways and the side streets until the route to your destination comes into view.

Get out a blank piece of paper. Draw a line down the middle, and on the left side, write MORE, and on the right side, write LESS. Now, peruse what you've discovered about your time style, your family's time styles, your fantasy schedule, your golden hours, and your current use of time. Write what you want more of in life in the MORE column. List even the far-fetched and impossible-seeming stuff. For example, "Travel to Indonesia" might appear here even if you don't have the budget or the vacation time to pull it off right this minute.

Then, identify the items that reliably drag you down. Write these things in the LESS column. Don't worry; you're not cutting anything yet. You're just drawing up the short list, and you can always change your mind later.

Keep checking in with your inner bus driver as you write your list. Your list is unique... it's based on YOU and your family. Resist the urge to let "shoulds" sneak onto your list. What's right for other people isn't necessarily right for you or your family. Cleaning, for example. Yes, you'd probably feel happier in a clean house. But if your inner bus driver is telling you there are more important priorities right now, put cleaning in the LESS column.

Also, don't let fear keep something off (or on) your list. If you're afraid to add or cut something from your schedule but your inner bus driver is quietly urging you in that direction, listen. Your inner bus driver is always smarter than your fear.

Throughout the next week or two, jot things on your More and Less List. Let it percolate. Change your mind, make amendments, play around. Write in pencil or pen. It's your list. It's your life.

Start Slow, Adjust As You Go

By now, you should have more insight into your family's "right" level of busy, what's important enough to merit space in your schedule, and what you might want to reduce or drop to free up more time. Your inner bus driver is pointed in the right direction. Now it's time to start the engine and get the bus rolling.

You're not going to remake your family's schedule overnight. The key is to start slowly, and adjust as you go. It takes trial and error to navigate toward balance. It takes time to get comfortable with the idea that by doing "less" you're actually inviting more goodness into your life. Certain commitments need to be seen through, while others aren't even on the horizon.

The important thing is to use your newfound insight as the lens and filter through which you manage your schedule from now on. Trusting yourself—letting your inner bus driver handle the windy road—can be scary at first, especially if you're still worried that you're somehow lowering your standards or jeopardizing your kids' opportunities. We know that today's environment doesn't exactly encourage "less" of anything.

This is a good time to reflect on the skills your children will gain from the time management work you're doing now. If you consider today's economic and social climate, we think you'll agree: the skills they'll gain from having more open time are as valuable (if not more) than anything they could learn in a class or on the soccer field:

- They'll have time to identify, explore, and pursue their interests, the first step in finding a life passion that could fuel their future.
- They'll be involved in meaningful ways with the work of family management, giving them direct experience with interdependence and teamwork.
- They'll learn to handle boredom (the best motivator for creativity).
- They'll get to play and be kids, a precursor to life balance as adults.
- They'll learn the importance of paying attention to their own inner bus drivers, which is central to handling growing responsibility, moral challenges, and peer pressure.

Scheduling Tools and Systems

All of our time philosophizing is fine, but it won't get you anywhere until you have concrete steps to take. To put your newfound enlightenment into action, you need tools and routines to turn time management into a daily habit.

Choose Your Tools

Lest you think we're all "there's no single right answer for everyone!" here's an absolute: *you must use a calendar and a to-do list.* These tools are the linchpins of time management because they free up headspace for problem solving rather than mundane memory jockeying.

Don't waste time searching for the Perfect Productivity Solution to magically steam iron the wrinkled fabric of your life. It doesn't exist. Simply do a quick survey of your options (or ask your friends for recommendations) and pick the one that seems most promising. It can be paper, electronic, a cheap wire-bound notebook and a pencil, a hundred-dollar "management system," a free app, or a stack of index cards. We don't care, as long as it is:

- Portable (it needs to be with you at all times)
- Something you find fun and/or are comfortable using
- Sharable with your partner (assuming you both participate in the family schedule and to-do list)

 Ali via the Minimalist Parenting blog: My husband and I both work full time. Our three- and five-year-olds are at prekindergarten and day care. We use Microsoft Outlook meeting requests to keep our schedules on track (which parent is out of town/who has to pick up kids, etc.). We have found it is extremely useful to combine our "work" and "home" calendars because work and home duties are so intertwined. Our calendars are also available on our smartphones. I schedule EVERYTHING, even travel time to and from events, and I include my husband's events if he is taking the kids somewhere (I code it yellow and mark it as free time so it does not mess up my calendar). I handle all to-dos for the kids and me and I use a rolling to-do list with all my work items, too. I save the list on Dropbox so it is available anywhere, and for any new items that pop into my brain I send an e-mail to my work e-mail address, which I know will get looked at and added to the list.

Put Your Tools into Action—Now

Put every date- and time-specific detail in your life into your calendar. Everything else goes into your to-do list. *Everything.* The places you hope to travel, the stuff you need at the hardware store, the phone calls you need to make. All the stuff you need or want to remember that doesn't have a specific time frame lives on your to-do list. (If your to-do items have due dates, you have some wiggle room as to whether to keep them on your to-do list or transfer them to your calendar. Choose whatever method makes most sense for you.)

Voilà, your mind now has more room to get creative and to rest. By off-loading the mental work of *remembering* your schedule and to-dos, you free up brain cells for the more important work of *organizing* and *managing* your life.

If you're new to calendar and to-do list management, tracking everything may initially leave you feeling a little cranky. In the beginning, this habit sucks up time and energy you probably feel you can't spare. But the more you use your tools, the more you'll come to trust and rely on them. You'll begin to notice patterns and recurring openings in your week, and how you might better use that time. Your mind will automatically begin breaking tasks and ideas into to-do list and calendar items, almost magically transforming you into a more organized and efficient person. But it's not magic—it's you. YOU are doing this!

Block Out Your Golden Hours

Earlier, you identified your golden hours—the hours you're most alert and productive. As much as you can, schedule your most creative and/ or challenging work during that time. These are the hours that deserve investment and protection. Whenever possible during this time, turn off the phone and social media, close the door, avoid scheduling meetings, and turn down the invitations for coffee or requests for attention. Challenge yourself to value your time enough to guard those hours, perhaps even with the help of your partner or a babysitter. Start slowly—even ten golden minutes per day—and expand from there.

Embrace "Autopilot"

With your golden hours spoken for, try to slot the more mundane stuff (filing, billing, errands, household administration) into less productive time. The best way to do that is to set up routines and recurring to-dos. Routines reduce any repetitive process into work you can do with your eyes practically closed. Recurring to-dos are helpful for building the habit of tending to dreaded minutia on a regular basis so it doesn't pile up and overwhelm you.

 I used to dread the menial nature of invoicing multiple clients every month, despite the obvious upside (getting paid!) and the fact that it didn't take all that long to do it. That changed once I set up each client invoice as a separate recurring monthly to-do item and got into the routine of setting aside an hour on the first of each month to handle invoicing. It feels great to check off a bunch of to-do items after I finish my invoicing every month. The same approach works great for recording my receipts and pay stubs so I'm not stuck with a huge pile of work right before tax time.

The reality is that so much of parenthood and domestic life is repetitive, boring, but necessary crap. Doing it is no fun, but the consequences of *not* doing it get in the way of Minimalist Parenting. The key is to create routines for handling the boring stuff: choose the process or chore that most annoys you and look for ways to break it down and make it more efficient. If you can, get other people involved.

 For me, the major culprit has always been laundry, also known as *the dreaded clothing monster*. There are so many steps in the process, all with potential to derail the train.

Every week, at least one of these things would happen: hampers would overflow, wet clothes mildewed in the washer, dry clothes wrinkled in the dryer, folded clothes sat forgotten in a laundry basket that never got taken upstairs, or, if it did, the clothes never made it into drawers (and got rifled through and unfolded). If, by some miracle, we did all of these things, at least one family member would still run out of underwear or socks. Guilt and frustration ensued.

We got the dreaded clothing monster under control by focusing attention on the specific steps involved in doing the laundry, and then simplifying them through routine and delegation:

- The kids empty their hampers into the laundry chute every day.
- Laundry runs while dinner is cooking every day (recurring to-do list item).
- Rael sorts and folds while watching evening TV. And now that I have a laundry buddy, I'm happy to pitch in and it gets done faster.
- The kids put away their own folded laundry whenever it appears in their rooms, and that job is tied to the start of TV and video game time (first the laundry, then the screen time).

Set an End Time

The work of parenting is endless. There's always one more thing to do. Accept it and bring sanity to your life by setting an end time to every day and "clocking out" on household minutia. Give yourself permission to switch into recreation and reconnection mode once your kids go to bed (or whenever feels right for you).

 jbrileyb via themotherhood.com: Is there a biological difference between men and women that makes it easier for men to disconnect [from household chores]? I used to resent my husband for it, but now I consider him a mentor of sorts. He just decides he's going to watch a hockey game, then sits down and does it. I'm realizing I should be *more* like him, not that he should be more like I am.

It's important to recognize that many working parents wrestle with the need to work at night, whether because of freelance/flexible work arrangements or because they've been out of the office tending to sick kids. In these cases, we suggest experimenting with different time arrangements so you can *still* set an end time—both for the household details and for your work.

Since I have more than a full-time workload and only part-time child care during the day, I rely on evenings for work time. Violet tends to go to bed an hour earlier than Laurel, and it's usually at this time that Jon steps in so I can retreat to my office. (Alternately, if Laurel wants company while engaging in a quiet activity such as reading or crafting, I'll bring my laptop down and work next to her.) This allows me to get some work time in before stopping for the night, at which point Jon and I take time to reconnect and/or I take some time to myself. It's the best way to unwind at the end of the day.

Some evenings the kids will wake up and interrupt you, or the world will conspire to complicate matters. It's inevitable, and it's okay. If you operate with (and communicate) an end time to each day, eventually the world will fall in line. Your kids will someday be old enough to realize "Oh, yeah. It's grown-up time," and they'll get their own glasses of water (especially if you keep cups and a step stool in the bathroom so they can reach). And they'll learn, from your example, about the importance of tending to responsibilities, relationships, and self-care.

Obviously, not every day will chart a perfect course nor will all of your to-dos get done. But you're now taking giant leaps toward minimalizing your schedule, so the most important, valuable, and fun stuff can shine. In the next chapter, we share even more tips for managing your time.

3

Time Management Tricks for Minimalists

Every parent's day is in a state of flux: one moment things are flowing nicely, and the next something comes along to upend everything. That's just the nature of things. With a minimalized schedule, not only are you better positioned to handle the inevitable surprises, you're more likely to be able to take advantage of spontaneous fun.

In this chapter, we share some of our best time management strategies. Try integrating one tip per week; see what feels right, and keep going from there.

Managing Your Time

While you're in the thick of your day, there are endless opportunities for distraction. Here are some tips for staying on track.

Don't Fall into the Multitasking Trap

We get that there's only so much interruption you can control (you can't exactly push the mute button on a toddler). But as much as you can, sharpen your focus. Turn off your e-mail, silence your phone, close Facebook and Twitter, and focus on the task at hand.

Tackle Your Hardest Thing First

We all have those nagging to-do items…some require focused time (e.g., generating a budget) whereas others come with emotional weight (e.g., a difficult phone call you need to make). Either way, procrastinating depletes your energy—every time your eyes hit that to-do list item and you don't address it, it slows your momentum.

Try this: start with the most onerous item on your to-do list. Often, you'll find that the task did not actually take that long, and you're immediately feeling freer and ready to rock the rest of your day because that burden is lifted.

Schedule "Serendipity Space"

When you're caught up in the routine of everyday life, it's easy to forget that you're modeling for your kids how to structure their time. Consider "padding" your activities with periods of quiet—"serendipity space"—where there is nothing to do and nowhere to go. That way, you can take advantage of the in-the-moment opportunities for puddle jumping or couch-cuddling that tend to get lost when there's always someplace to be five minutes ago.

Take Advantage of "In-Between Minutes"

The more you use your calendar, the more you'll notice little snatches of time throughout your day that are too short for anything substantial, but are perfect for one- to five-minute tasks and/or distraction breaks. The secret is to have those little tasks queued up in your to-do list so you can take advantage of the in-between minutes. Good "in-between" tasks include:

- Making phone calls
- Checking social media
- Responding to email (see our three-touch e-mail rule in chapter 5)

- Doing self-care tasks that fall by the wayside (e.g., nail filing, stretching)
- Tidying up, even a single drawer or surface
- Sorting the mail
- Filing papers (or, better, shredding and recycling them)
- Looking ahead in your calendar and to-do list to see where you could benefit from a little planning (for example, noting a birthday the following week so you remember to put a card on your shopping list)

Tweak Your Scheduling Style

We all continue to evolve in our relationships and realize new things about one another; sometimes these differences come to bear when the system reaches pressure points. Be open to tweaking your scheduling style, either to reach a compromise or to improve life.

 Jon and I were married for ten years before we explicitly talked about our different time styles. My tendency was to schedule things ahead of time because I preferred to handle RSVPs immediately, while Jon preferred to wait to make decisions based on how he was feeling in the moment.

As we worked to find a balance between the two approaches amid the seemingly never-ending tide of professional and personal commitments, I started experimenting with Jon's approach to last-minute planning (stopping short of being rude to the host). And you know what? I found it incredibly liberating. It allowed me to make decisions based on how I was feeling at the time (rather than simply being driven by "shoulds") and it also eased the scheduling tension between Jon and me.

Pause Before Saying Yes

Don't say yes to things you and your family don't want to do. Obligation is a difficult beast to battle, but really, what's worse: declining an invite or task, or gritting your teeth and muddling through with "I don't want to do this" mojo? Beyond the basic things you *must* do, reserve your energy for the things that make you feel happy and excited. No excuses necessary. Simply respond with "Thank you for asking/inviting us, but we're unable to do it/attend."

 My brother-in-law Josh is an excellent baker. After an argument with his partner, he decided to make brownies as a peace offering. He didn't realize it while he was baking, but apparently he was still angry about their argument because his brownies—usually moist, chewy, and full of gooey love and goodness—came out all burnt and nasty. He and his partner ended up having a good laugh over this, dubbing them the "angry brownies." Jon and I took this story to heart. We avoid doing things for each other while still carrying resentment because the results always come out burnt.

Managing Time with Others

In the modern parenting quest to do it all, there's a dissonant tendency to do it alone. Many of us put too much pressure on ourselves to forge ahead solo, feeling that asking for help is tantamount to admitting failure.

In fact, asking for help is a sign of strength—and a gift to yourself and those around you—especially when you can avoid becoming a festering martyr (Christine used to be President of the Festering Martyr Club). Household chores are more agreeable when your family does them together, and you may develop new and unexpected friendships (and chip away at isolation) when you lean on other parents for help.

Partnering with Your Partner

If you're coparenting, using time well begins with your partnership. Managing a family together is a tricky dance, but it's the most important step toward encouraging a sane household and an intimate parenting partnership. Here are some key tactics to help you support one another as you both manage the family "bucket" of time.

Share the Work

Dividing the labor too firmly can result in you and your partner operating in separate worlds, coexisting but rarely overlapping. Even the most flexible of couples can fall into rigid roles because, in the moment, it often feels easier to go with what has worked in the past. But we encourage you to frequently swap parenting jobs for the following reasons:

- Sometimes you'll want a break from a particular task and you might resent it if you feel as though you don't have permission or the opportunity to get that break.
- Dividing tasks too strictly complicates matters when one parent isn't available. The parent who is away should be able to spend her time focused on the purpose of the trip, not on whether the parent at home knows how to handle the kid-related details. Meanwhile, the parent at home should simply be able to tick off routine tasks for what they are—routine tasks—instead of worrying about doing the job according his partner's standards or feeling incompetent because he doesn't know how to proceed.
- Kids need to see *both* parents as people on whom they can rely. Let go of expectations around "job perfection" ("job done" is perfectly fine!). Shoot for respectful acceptance of each other's talents and weaknesses, clear communication, close collaboration, and permeable boundaries between your respective areas of responsibility.
- Finally, if you literally job share (as Asha and Rael now approach laundry, described in chapter 2), you can find ways to make mundane work fun. Or at the very least a point of reconnection.

Give Each Other Transition Time

It's the end of the workday and you've hit the zone of intense parenting. One of you has been home with the kids and needs a break while the other is coming off a long day at the office. Or both of you are flying through the door from work, trying to find a child-safe place to drop your personal effects while getting the update from the sitter. In both cases, your kids are clamoring for your attention. You hurtle into a couple of hours of dinner, baths, stories, games—trying to reconnect with your kids while thinking through the household chores still left to do while ticking through some outstanding work to-dos. Phew. Our recommendation: give each other some transition time.

Jon and I have found that we can be more present and calm during the evening with Laurel and Violet when we give each other transition time at the end of the day. It doesn't need to be long or involved. All Jon wants is ten minutes upstairs to crank some tunes, change his clothes, and take a few deep breaths before the girls jump all over him. Since I work out of our home, my preference is to leave the house, however briefly. There have been days when Jon has gotten home a little early and encouraged me to use that unexpected buffer to fit in a short run, which is one of my favorite ways to clear my head and change my scenery.

Divide the Work in the Way That Makes Sense for You

While we recommend that each parent learns how to handle the basic domestic and child care tasks, we also suggest dividing tasks based on skill, interest, and schedules, not on a fifty-fifty definition of "what's fair."

Jesser of jesser.org, via the Minimalist Parenting blog: I tend to do a bit more of the cooking, because I enjoy it, and my husband takes on more yard work. I organize our finances and pay bills. He maintains our house. In general, he is the one who gets up in the middle of the night. Because I work outside the home four days per week and he works at home five days per week, his schedule is a bit more flexible than mine (he can catch an extra half hour of sleep in the morning, for instance). He also goes back to sleep more easily after being up in the middle of the night. I take over the whole ship when he is out of town for work.

Tiffany via the Minimalist Parenting blog: I work from home very early every day, so my husband will fix breakfast and make lunches. I am able to get the boys off the bus and take care of dinner and the cooking on the weekends (because I enjoy it). This system works very well for us. He also cleans the bathrooms, and I take care of vacuuming and dusting.

Free Up Alone Time
In addition to general family time and some one-on-one time with the kids (splitting up for errands and activities that are better suited to each kid works well here), alone time—for self-care or special projects—helps contribute to a happy partnership.

Jon and I try to build "swap time" into every weekend. Essentially, we take turns each having a couple of hours to ourselves while the other person spends time with the kids. We've found swap time to be one of the best ways to recharge and feel ready to parent.

Use Your Calendar to Your Advantage
In chapter 2, we talked about the importance of using a calendar. The benefit of a shared electronic calendar is that it allows you both to be more aware of how much the other is handling. It's also helpful to sit down and look at the family calendar together, as a constant flow of logistical e-mail and conversation tends to overwhelm everyone.

Morra Aarons-Mele of WeAreWomenOnline.com and TheMissionList.com: My husband and I operate on a mantra shared by a very wise therapist we saw before we got married: In the marriage, you have the love relationship, and you have the "Corporation." A successful marriage requires taking time to keep your love and family relationship together (fun, dates, kid time, sex, etc.). But you also need to manage the Corporation (schedule, finances, child care, health care, lawn care, pet care, etc.).

We have two key household documents to manage the Corporation: a budget spreadsheet in which we track monthly fixed costs and match them to our actual spending, and a calendar that we share with our nanny and my mom. Since my husband and I both travel a lot, the calendar has to be tightly managed. We literally schedule monthly check-ins—sometimes at our favorite breakfast place—to review the calendar and general household budget. On Sunday nights, we try to go over the week's calendar.

Create Routines Together

Model simple and consistent routines for your kids that will also make family and grown-up time together more enjoyable:

 Kym of coffeemomma.blogspot.com, via the Minimalist Parenting blog: My husband and I have only two firm rules. Number one: family dinner. Every night. No phones. We sit down at the table together, even if it's just leftovers, and we talk. If the phone rings, we let it go (unless we are waiting for news on a family member who is sick or struggling, obviously, but that's rare). Number two: my kids have a bedtime. They are both in bed and asleep by 8 p.m. Evenings are for my husband and me. We talk, we watch TV together, or we just hang out and read together on the couch. It's our time, and it's crucial to us to touch base each night and check in with each other. We're constantly adjusting our parenting strategy, and we do a lot of "this isn't working...." course changes. These two rules are so important to us. It's how we keep our sanity and make sure our kids (and the two of us) feel loved.

Strengthening Your Community

By now you probably have gathered that we're all about asking for help. If you're fortunate enough to live near family members who are also willing babysitters, that's wonderful. But there's an entire community around you—friends, neighbors, and parents at your child's school—that can become an interdependent network of support and camaraderie.

When parents reach out to each other for help, *everyone* benefits—not just the help-ee. The helper gets the satisfaction of doing something for a friend, as well as an invitation to a deeper, more mutually helpful friendship. As chores bond families, mutual favors cement neighborhoods and communities. Whether it's swapping organizing services with a friend (it's always easier to organize other people's stuff), setting up a neighborhood dinner club, trading babysitting or playdates, or ride sharing, there are plenty of options that create fun for your kids, build community, and reduce the load on you.

 It was a miraculous day when drop-off playdates became a possibility. I have a wonderful network of local parents with whom I enjoy socializing, but you get to a point where, while the kids are off doing their own thing, it really would be most productive for the parents to also be doing their own thing.

I was a little hesitant the first time I asked a fellow parent for help. I was on a huge deadline and my life would be made enormously easier if the parent of one of Laurel's friends could pick her up from school and have her for a playdate for a couple of hours. When I asked, the mom said, "Oh yes, please! It's actually easier for *me* when my daughter has a friend over. She's happier and I can also get some stuff done around the house."

That one hesitant question opened a door of reciprocity that we now regularly enjoy with the families of Laurel's school friends. We swap playdates, share rides to soccer, and help each other with meals and other details when someone is struggling. Tapping into, and being a part of, this community is about as close as it comes to that "village" for which we all long.

Outsourcing

Sometimes the easiest way to do a nagging job is to pay someone else to do it. It may feel a little uncomfortable to swallow your pride, accept that you can't do it all, place a dollar value on your time, and wrestle with the concept of hiring help, but the upsides are clear. If you're in the midst of a "time famine" and outsourcing will help you recoup time and reduce stress, it's worth it. Not to mention that you will support local businesses (and, residually, the families of those employees) in the process.

Think about the responsibilities that you alone can do. Focus on those and outsource other tasks that are not you-specific, as you are able.

Give Your Kids Chores

When your children are babies, *they* are the work that needs to be shared. But sooner than you expect, kids grow into capable members of the household. As soon as possible, open up your schedule by giving your kids chores and responsibilities.

Why Chores Are Important

Involving children in home management may seem like more work at first, but it's as close to a parenting "sure thing" as you can get. Not only will you gradually reduce your workload, you'll teach your kids practical, esteem-building skills they'll use for the rest of their lives.

There's something subtler at work here, too. When kids understand they are crucial members of the family "team," it brings the entire family closer together. Not only do they gain confidence from their accomplishments, they come to appreciate their parents' work as well.

How to Assign Chores

A number of parents we've spoken with feel surprisingly nervous about giving their kids chores. They're overwhelmed by the number of chore "methodologies" out there and wonder which works best, and they dread what they assume will be inevitable arguments from their kids.

When chores are introduced as a regular and expected part of growing up, they're *no big deal*. Don't worry if your kids hesitate to jump onto the chore bandwagon. Few kids clap with glee when asked to clean their rooms or empty the dishwasher. Learning that some work is mundane but important—and must be done anyway—is fine preparation for independence.

If necessary, reorder your daily rhythm so free time happens *after* chores are done. "Sure, you can watch TV after your chores are done," has a different ring than "You can't watch TV until your chores are done."

Julie Pippert of theartfulflower.blogspot.com, via themotherhood.com: My kids have trouble in the morning. Not morning people. So, together, we write down their chores on a chart and they illustrate it with pictures. Later, they can check the chart to make sure they are getting through it all.

Another option: tie chores to allowance. For many families, this works well; for others, it takes away from the expectation of family responsibility. We discuss allowance further in chapter 6.

Start Small

Even letting young children wipe down the table or pass out the napkins before dinner is a good start. Let them know that their work is important to the family, and educate them about the work you do for the family as well. Demonstrate your confidence in their ability to handle increasingly challenging tasks.

Be Cheerful

It's not as crazy as it sounds; sometimes the pitch makes all the difference. If you approach kids warily about chores because you are dreading an argument, they likely will sense the negotiability of the situation. Instead, use a matter-of-fact tone when you assign the chore du jour and point out that you'll be doing your own work right alongside them.

I explained the importance of chores to my daughter like this: when she gets a little older, she's going to fly…all over the world. But she's going to need strong wings to do it. Every time she does a job or solves her own problem, she's strengthening her wings.
My son got a slightly different spin: I framed chores as "move-out skills" his future college roommates would respect and appreciate. Neither is enthusiastic about chores, but at least they understand how their work fits into the bigger picture of growth.

When Possible, Offer Choices (But Not Too Many)
So many meltdowns can be avoided when you give kids choice and control. Letting kids choose between two chore-based responses ("Would you like to set the table *or* pick up the toys in the living room?") means they're positioned to make a choice instead of to say no. (They might *still* say no, but you'll be in a better position to redirect their attention.)

 I used to call Sam the "Choice C kid." If we gave him a choice between A and B, he would choose C. This frustrated us at the time, but for the most part we stuck to our guns, doing our best to communicate the non-negotiability of the choices. It took years for him to accept our roles as family leaders, but we can now see how much he respects our decisions (he comes to us for advice all the time). Now that he's older, there are more opportunities for his "outside the box" thinking to shine. It's one of his great strengths.

Focus First on Effort, Then on Results
Kids are on their own developmental timetables, so if your child doesn't seem to get it right away, that's okay. Persistence pays off. Any effort in the right direction is good.

Discovering the strategies and systems that work best for your family will be an evolving process, but you'll get there—especially now that you know there's a team around you to help.

TIME-SAVING TECH PICKS

A smartphone can be a busy parent's best friend when it comes to staying organized and saving time. We asked tech savvy moms Kristen Chase and Liz Gumbinner, publishers of CoolMomTech.com, to share their top time-saving smartphone apps:

- **Orchestra**. Ditch your paper to-do lists. The Orchestra app not only allows you to organize by time frame (like yesterday!) or personal designation, but also lets you e-mail invites, reminders, and bill notices to merge them into your to-do list. It's seriously genius. Pair it with using voice recognition software, (so smart for busy parents who rarely have a free hand) to assign tasks to people who don't have Orchestra. Just dictate a reminder and send it directly to the recipient via text message or e-mail.

- **Dropbox**. Although many people use Dropbox to share large files online, this free service (and app) also helps you organize your important documents, photos, wish lists and more in shared, password-protected folders on your computer. Just imagine life with no more calls from Grandma about that dance recital video you forgot to send. If she has the Dropbox password, she can see it without you having to lift a finger.

- **Evernote**. Think of Evernote as your virtual bulletin board, allowing you to clip, save, and organize everything—from your favorite websites and recipes to design inspiration for your kids' bedrooms—all in one place. The super-simple interface lets you upload the app and start getting organized without having to read an instruction manual or snooze your way through a video tutorial.

- **Cozi**. Parents rave about the Cozi Management system. This veritable command central allows you to manage multiple people's schedules, sync calendars and to-do lists, and even send your grocery list right to your cell phone so you never forget the toilet paper again. All your family members have access so you can input changes as they come to you, thus alerting everyone about the updates.

HOW TO GET TO FLEX

All parents know how critical workplace flexibility is to family life. But it can be extremely challenging to figure out how to achieve it. We asked the brilliant Ellen Galinsky, president of the Families and Work Institute (familiesandwork.org) and author of Mind in the Making, *to share her top tips for achieving workplace flexibility:*

Most of us as parents feel starved for time. In fact, we call it a "time famine" in our studies. According to Families and Work Institute's (FWI) nationally representative study of the U.S. workforce: 75 percent of employees say they don't have enough time with their children, up from 66 percent in 1992; 63 percent of employees say they don't have enough time for their spouses or partners, up from 50 percent in 1992, and 60 percent of employees don't have enough time for ourselves, up from 55 percent in 2002—the first time FWI asked this question.

Having flexibility helps a lot. Not surprisingly, 87 percent say that flexibility is essential or very important when looking for a new job, but only one in four of us currently has flexibility. So how do we change this? Here are some tips in approaching your supervisor to ask for flexibility:

- **Find out what your organization offers in flexibility, either formally or informally.** More than workflex programs and policies, find out what your organization's experiences with flexibility have been. What has worked? What hasn't? Why? As you think about approaching your supervisor, it is important to be ready to counter any bad experiences that he or she might have had in the past.
- **Find champions in your organization.** It is always better if there are others working with you who want your organization to become more flexibile for business reasons. These people should be respected and it is always good to have unexpected messengers. These people can give you advice and advocate for you as you prepare to talk with your supervisor.
- **Make a business case in approaching your supervisor.** While it is tempting to put your needs first, the most successful proposals to supervisors talk about how flexibility can help the organization address a business challenge.
- **Outline a few options for flexibility.** Rather than approaching your supervisor with just one option, think of several types of flexibility that might help you. Be prepared to address how your work will get done.
- **Suggest a trial period and propose some metrics to assess whether this arrangement is working.** Supervisors are always more likely to go along with a pilot rather than a "forever" arrangement.

In a study I did several years ago, I asked a nationally representative group of children from the third to the twelfth grades a "one wish" question: "If you had one wish to improve the way your mother's or your father's work affects your life, what would that wish be?"

While most parents thought their children would wish for more time together, that wasn't what the largest proportion of children wished. If they had one wish, they wished their parents would be less tired and less stressed. So remember that while flexibility can give you more time together, it is what you are like in that time with your kids that matters most. If you are tired and stressed (and we all are), find ways to try to deal with the stress and not let it spill over on your children.

4

A New Way to Think About Your Stuff

In November 2008, around the time many of us likely were fretting over not having enough counter space, cabinets, and kitchen gadgets to pull off Thanksgiving dinner, the *New York Times* ran an interview with Mark Bittman—journalist, food writer, and author of *How to Cook Everything*.

In the feature, Bittman shared how he cooks in the modest kitchen of his Manhattan flat—forgoing common tools such as a toaster or food processor due to space limitations. It was impressive and inspiring to think of a foodie of his caliber getting by without such seemingly basic kitchen tools. (Incidentally, for many years he wrote a weekly *New York Times* column called "The Minimalist.")

But not everyone can (or wants to) forgo the metaphorical toaster. Before you begin the task of editing your stuff, it helps to take stock of what you might want to keep…and why. In this chapter, we take a moment to think about why clutter piles up in the first place. The answer is different for everyone. Therefore, choices about what to keep, what to toss or donate, and how to maintain a clutter-free environment differ as well.

From there, we'll help you shift your perspective about your stuff so you can clear the decks (literally) as you minimalize your way to a happier, more relaxed physical and emotional space.

What Purpose Is Your Clutter Serving?

In no area of family life does the first key of Minimalist Parenting—make room for remarkable—translate so literally. Most of us feel happier and clearer in more open and organized environments, but getting there can be tricky for reasons that have nothing to do with the stuff itself. The reality is that *physical* decluttering is easier when you're aware of the *emotional* clutter that goes along with it. We'd like to help you navigate the *whys* of clutter so you can acknowledge and move past them.

It Fills an Emotional "Hole"

On the surface, "stuff" seems so tangible and straightforward, doesn't it? But our relationship with stuff can be complex. For example, have you ever felt—as Christine has at times—the need to compensate for the things that were missing from your own childhood? Or that you buy stuff for your kids that addresses your own needs or insecurities?

 My tendency toward clutter comes directly from my thrifty, practical upbringing. One of two phrases is behind every bit of clutter in my house: "It's perfectly good" and "It may come in handy someday." I feel wasteful (and a bit spoiled and entitled) when I get rid of something I think we may use in the future.

It may help to keep these ideas in mind as you navigate through (and past) the emotional reasons behind physical clutter:

You're Not a Bad Person for Having "Issues"

Many of our automatic reactions to stuff were formed when we were children ourselves, so try not to get hung up on your hang-ups. You're doing the best you can and you're working hard to grow and improve. It's a gradual process and you'll probably stumble along the way, and that's okay.

Your Child Does Not Know Your Backstory
When you're wrestling with the emotions around clutter, it's easy to forget that your kids don't know your backstory. It's helpful to keep this in mind because your reactions (anger, sadness, frustration) can be confusing to your kids, who are still learning to get a handle on their own (considerable) wants.

It Covers Up Social Insecurity

There is so much pressure on parents to buy, buy, buy. Other parents are buying (right?), and we want to look good (or at least not bad) in their eyes. We feel a sense of obligation to provide our kids with the best, including the things we never had. Millions of savvy marketing dollars are spent activating our parental insecurities and fears in order to manufacture need.

When I was pregnant, those "must-have" nursery lists were so hard to resist! I knew on some level there was no way all that stuff was necessary (people raised babies for millennia before the Diaper Genie was invented), but I also felt a basic anxiety that I was shortchanging my kid if I didn't spring for top-quality bedding or a stroller with all the bells and whistles.

It's hard to listen to your inner bus driver when you're assaulted by the noise of social pressures, but that's where the path to clarity begins. As you contend with real and imagined social pressures, try to remember:

You're Not Alone
Other parents are probably feeling what you are feeling. Actually, we *know* they are because we've heard this message loud and clear in our online communities.

It's Your Chance to Shine
By acting on your values, you are setting an example—for your kids and for other parents—that acting in service of your family system takes conviction and strength.

You Are Smarter Than You Think

During periods of self-doubt, it's difficult to remember that you are completely competent to make your own decisions. Remember that you are driving the bus. You can do this.

Thinking About Stuff Differently

Minimalist Parenting is not an exercise in deprivation. You can still enjoy shopping, decorating, and aesthetics. The trick is to focus on *worth*. If you use it or you love it, it's worth making space for it in your life.

I have a silly cell phone charm that serves no specific purpose. I bought it in a tourist shop in San Francisco's Chinatown while visiting with my family. It was my kids' first visit to Chinatown and we had so much fun playing with the toys we found in the stalls lining the crowded sidewalks. That cheap little trinket brings back happy memories every time I see it dangling from my coat pocket or purse. In someone else's life, that cell phone charm might classify as throwaway clutter. But I treasure it.

Before we get into the nuts and bolts of decluttering, here are a few ways to look at your stuff with new eyes.

Embrace a Small Living Space

When given the space, the tendency for most families is to fill it. Why not embrace *less* space (typically the opposite of what people do when deciding on homes) in order to control "stuff creep"?

Carla Naumburg via the Minimalist Parenting blog: We have a small house, with a corner in our living room designated for toys. We have a bookshelf and some bucket shelving in that area. If the toys don't fit in there, then we know it's time to get rid of a few! My daughters (ages two and three-and-a-half) put their toys away every night while I sweep. Because we have a small house, it feels pretty manageable.

Rachel Shipp of healthynaturaleasyish.com, via the Minimalist Parenting blog: A house larger than you need just leads to a state of serious disorganization. When my husband and I moved into our moderate-sized house, we almost doubled our square footage and doubled the number of bedrooms. There was no need to worry about organization, because there was space for everything. As we acquired new stuff, we just put it where it would fit. Five years and three kids later, I regret that lack of organization. Every. Single. Day. Especially since my time is so limited for fixing the problem...I really think when it comes to house size, less is more. Less space leads very naturally to more organization.

Consider Leaving Empty Space Empty

In tandem with the less (square footage) is more concept, there's a case to be made for empty space. The tendency is to think of empty space as something negative: lonely, unused, even devoid of love. But empty space is actually the opposite; it's a necessary positive that allows the surroundings to shine. It's the physical equivalent of "making room for remarkable."

Rael has helped me come to appreciate the beauty of empty space. I used to consider his taste rather spartan, but I now see that his mind works better with less visual clutter, and so does mine (and the kids').

Think About the Ways Your Stuff Can Move Forward

It may sound a little lofty, but your stuff may have a higher purpose to serve. Think about the different and positive ways your stuff can move out into the universe, whether it's via donation, selling, or sharing with loved ones.

Only by thinking about how my stuff might be more useful to someone else can I chip away at my resistance to decluttering. I also find this helps my kids let go of their outgrown toys. Sam has an entrepreneurial streak and is always planning a yard sale or a trip to the used bookstore to sell his stuff. Mirabai (who's attached to the memories associated with her toys and clothes) takes great comfort in knowing they will help another child.

Remember That Less Stuff Feels More Special

It's the old saw about quantity versus quality. Even kids can discover that having less stuff makes the remaining stuff feel more special.

Laurel gets very attached to stuff. I don't think it's due to fear of not having enough, but because she develops sentimental attachments and also is concerned that she will hurt the feelings of whoever gave an item to her if the person learns that she gave the item away. I get this, but I recently reached my breaking point over her stuffed animals. Yes, perhaps some of my own issues were creeping in here (I didn't receive my first stuffed animal until I was five years old, following a tonsillectomy) but there was just too much. I decided it was finally time to talk to Laurel about donation.

When I first raised the topic, Laurel responded with the expected distress. I shared my discomfort over her abundance of stuffed animals given that she played so little (or not at all) with most of them and many kids have no stuffed animals. I told her that I had found a website that coordinates donations of gently used stuffed animals. She paused for a few minutes, clearly turning this over in her mind (she's very empathetic and we've done many new toy donations in the past), and then she nodded her mind and said, "OK Mom, let's do it!"

Laurel and I proceeded to declutter her stuffed animals. It was easier with the toys for which she couldn't remember the giver, but in general, she handled it incredibly well. In about ten to fifteen minutes we had moved most of the landslide into several large trash bags and what was left clearly were the Chosen Ones—each beloved and with a unique history.

Laurel then proceeded to arrange this group carefully on the floor next to her bed—facing them out so she could see them all and find them whenever she wanted to gather an assembly. When she finished, she stepped back and laughed. I asked her what was so funny and she said, "You know, Mom, I thought this would be really hard but I'm not feeling bad about any of the stuffed animals I'm giving away. And actually, having less of them makes all of these ones feel more special."

Exactly.

Acquire Mindfully

Have you ever gone to a store intending to buy one thing but walking out with ten? Yeah, us too. But before you drop something into your physical or virtual shopping cart, ask yourself: Do I really need this? Is this special? Is this worth the effort of making space for in my home...and in my life?

Recast yourself as a curator of special things rather than as an easily swayed consumer who pounces on purchases due to peer pressure or fear of scarcity (e.g., they're on sale). We get into greater detail about assessing value in chapter 6.

Used = Good

Some people have a prejudice against secondhand anything. We say: that prejudice is worth challenging. While you might want to draw the line in certain places (e.g., underwear), secondhand items are usually fine. In fact, they're often more than fine:

- You'll pay less for well-made items that last
- Kids outgrow clothes and toys so quickly
- Plenty of baby gear has a limited-use window

My second pregnancy came as a big surprise. After several years of being open to expanding our family with no result, I came to terms with the possibility that I was no longer fertile and donated almost all of our baby goods. Of course, I found myself pregnant a couple of months later. When my girlfriend Heidi offered to host a baby shower, I asked if she would be willing to coordinate a secondhand baby shower. Why? Because I'm a big fan of recycling kid stuff and because I had many friends who were done having babies and had already asked if they could pass things along (I believe their words were, "Please borrow this and never, ever give it back!"). Since then, a lot of people have asked me how to coordinate a secondhand baby shower. Here's the how-to:

- **Make a list of things you actually need.** Because it had been so long since I'd had baby gear on my mind, I referred to one of those (absurd, in my opinion) "must-have" baby gear registry lists with about 1,382 things on it and narrowed it down to the absolute basics. Hand this list over to your shower host, along with the guest list.
- **Query for hand-me-downs.** One option is to float the list to friends and let the hand-me-downs fall where they may, as it were. However, if you or the host want to take a more organized approach, you can do what Heidi did, which was have people respond to her regarding what they were bringing, in order to prevent duplicates.
- **Be okay with other things. Or nothing at all!** Most of all, I wanted to spend time with my friends, particularly because the shower ended up including a remarkable collection of amazing women from different parts of my life. I truly did not care if people brought things, as long as they brought themselves! There also were attendees who were long done with kids and no longer had items to hand down. To make people comfortable, Heidi indicated in the invitation that people were welcome to simply come and hang out; if they wanted to bring something other than hand-me-downs, gift cards or diapers were handy, easy options.
- **Keep it simple.** Heidi is incredibly generous and she catered a

lovely spread of sweet and savory items. However, it's also totally fine to keep things simple. If you'd rather not serve a meal, schedule the shower for a between-meal hour, for example, 2 to 4 p.m., and offer beverages and light snacks.

- **Coordinate a departure plan.** Depending on your haul (and how pregnant you are), you might need help at departure time. In addition to large items such as a jogging stroller and crib mattress, I also received four crates (!) of secondhand clothing and toys, among other things. I definitely needed help getting it all home!

Experiment With Going Without

Every now and then you'll find yourself without access to your daily comforts, whether due to loss, breakage, or being away from home. Hold off on replacing things right away; you may find you can minimalize things you thought you couldn't live without!

 We went through a bizarre high maintenance season in our home. We needed to put in a sump pump. We had multiple plumbing issues. So when the ice maker and microwave died, Jon and I decided to experiment with going without (both to save money and yet another trip to Home Depot). The ice maker was easy—it's not that difficult to fill ice trays with water.

I was a little more hesitant to lose the convenience of the microwave, but replacing it was a bigger hassle (it's an over-the-stove unit attached to some cabinets). We agreed to go for a month without it; if we felt we still needed it after that month, we'd replace it.

The first week took a little getting used to but we were soon in the groove with using the stove or the toaster. Added bonus? The microwave (which we left in place because it would be a hassle to remove it) now serves as extra storage space.

Clutter clearly isn't just physical, it's got emotional talons too. But now that you've started to identify the *whys* of your clutter, you're hopefully thinking about your stuff a little differently. In the next chapter, we'll share strategies to help you minimalize the physical clutter.

5

From Clutter to Curation: Minimalizing Your Home

You know that *ahhhh* feeling when you spend time in a tidy, organized room? Space that contains just what it needs to be functional and comfortable—but no more—lets you relax and think in a way you just can't in a cluttered environment. The same is true for kids: when the playroom (or homework desk or art project area) is clear and only a few toys or supplies are on display, creative thinking and imagination have room to run.

You're about to transform your home into that retreat. It won't happen overnight and it won't happen without effort, but it will happen and we'll help you get there. In this chapter, we'll show you how to declutter your home, organize what's left, keep it maintained, and, most importantly, get the whole family involved.

Decluttering: How to Unstuff

As families grow, so—typically—does the clutter. Stuff multiplies like rabbits, and empty spaces fill with crap (yes, crap). Kids complain about having nothing to play with, when they are actually overwhelmed by the volume of toys available. No more! It's time to cut the crap and declutter. (Don't worry about organizing for now—when you declutter first you won't waste time organizing stuff you'll ultimately toss.)

Getting Started

The mere *idea* of decluttering can be overwhelming. We get it, which is why we lay out a series of small steps for getting started. Whether you have an hour or just fifteen minutes, you can make a difference. Here's how to get the ball rolling:

Grab Your Supplies

Assemble your decluttering receptacles. We recommend: (1) a large trash bag for **trash**; (2) a paper grocery bag for **recyclables**; (3) another large trash bag for **donations**; and (4) a storage bin for the **remaining items** that need to be put away elsewhere in the house.

Identify Your Target Area

With your supplies in hand, identify your target area. Start with a high-traffic area or the area that bugs you most (e.g., toy/crap pile in the corner of the living room) so immediate gratification can further motivate your decluttering efforts.

Set Reachable Goals Based on Your Time

Set yourself up to succeed. Instead of saying "I'm going to organize the basement today!" start with a tangible goal you can complete in the block of time you have available (e.g., a single rack of shelves in the basement, or even a single shelf).

I tend to get overwhelmed by all the decisions decluttering forces me to make. Should I sell this item or give it away? Where should this go? Do I really need it? Because I can become paralyzed by indecision, I need to break decluttering projects into small bits. I either set the timer for ten-minute decluttering sessions or I declutter one small space at a time. Or, I enlist a buddy to help.

Have an Exit Strategy

End your decluttering session with the reward of admiring your newly opened-up space...not the pile of stuff you now need to figure out how to distribute. Leave time to get the stuff you declutter *out of your house.* Ideally, you'll take it directly to the donation station, but at a minimum, clear space in your garage or car trunk for future sale, donation, or giveaway. We'll talk more specifically about finding new homes for your stuff later in the chapter.

Getting into a Decluttering Rhythm

Now that you have crossed the threshold from "thinking about" to "doing," here are some tips for getting into a decluttering rhythm.

Be Objective

Measure the worth of your belongings against objective questions. On our blog, MaryJo of respacedpdx.com suggested the following excellent benchmark: "Would I pay money to replace it if it were lost in a fire?" Asha's version is "Would I take this to my retirement studio in SoHo?" (We talk more about how to assess worth and value in chapter 6.) Go fast: If you can't quickly identify a meaningful or useful purpose for an item, move it out.

Start with the Big and/or Expensive Stuff

One way to start off with a bang is to focus on donating or selling high-value pieces and large items. The money and/or space you gain will motivate you to keep going. Something else to consider: when you give items to friends or family who need them, instead of selling them, you'll feel good about helping someone you love *and* you'll clear space right away *and* you'll save the time and energy it takes to coordinate transactions.

After buying a streamlined music system for our home, Jon and I were looking to unload a small stereo system. I initially listed the stereo on Craigslist, but at that particular point in time I found myself overwhelmed with dealing with more e-mail and people trying to haggle down our asking price. I conveyed this to Jon and he said, "Don't spend another minute on it. Why don't we ask Thomas [the college-bound son of our next door neighbor] if he wants it?" When we offered the stereo to Thomas, he asked how much we wanted for it and we said we'd simply love for him to take it. He looked surprised and happy, and we felt happy too.

Avoiding the Nostalgia Stall-Out

You're trying to declutter but you've hit a wall. Perhaps several walls, in the form of boxes of letters from old flames, your first basketball trophy, expensive camping gear from when you used to love camping (ten years ago), and piles of baby paraphernalia.

If nostalgia is bogging you down, here are some tips for honoring it while maintaining your decluttering momentum.

Challenge the Nostalgia

Nostalgia is natural, but the box of letters from ex-boy/girlfriends? Not necessary (or productive). Nor is every holiday card and letter, unless something extremely meaningful is written inside. Your personal journals, on the other hand, might be worth saving. Think in terms of your living history; keep select items that will paint a picture of who you were at different phases of your life and discard the rest.

Mirabai is extremely sentimental, so culling her possessions involves lots of resistance and worry that she'll lose happy associations. We talk about the difference between objects and memories, and that the two don't need to remain attached. We take pictures of favorite toys and store them in a digital album; the very act of "keeping" something—even if it's just an image—usually gives her enough acknowledgment and closure that she can part with her belongings. This is also a good way to handle your child's art projects and building block creations. If you're feeling ambitious, you could even create a photo book out of the results.

Use Your Reaction As a Benchmark

Unless you have an immediate positive reaction to an item, you can probably let it go. If you have a decidedly *negative* reaction to an item, definitely get rid of it. Removing toxicity from your life = good. You're making room for remarkable!

Don't Save Things "Just In Case"

One thing that became clear to Christine following her secondhand baby shower (see chapter 4) was that she is lucky to be blessed by abundance. Thanks to her friends, she was able to prepare for Violet's arrival at basically zero expense. It also enabled her to get past the nostalgia of Violet's outgrown things and whether or not she should save things "just in case":

I have no idea whether I'm done growing babies. However, there is one thing I am certain of, and it's that I can't bear to hold on to baby things I may or may not need in the future when there are people who need them *now*.

Our stuffed animal donation (which I described in chapter 4) was a bit of a wake-up call for me. We collected so much and I felt so much lighter—emotionally and physically—knowing that these items would make their way into the hands of kids in need. Not too long after donating the stuffed animals, I heard that my town was coordinating a toy/clothing/gear drive for local families in need. I was determined to identify items that I *could* use *if* we have another baby and donate them to people who needed them *now*. I took ten minutes to scour the basement and collected a stroller, a Snap N Go stroller base, a wooden high chair, and two baby play gyms. All of these items were handed down to me and it seemed only fitting to hand them down to someone else.

Create a "Last Stop"

If you can't decide whether or not to let something go (and it's slowing you down or amping up your anxiety), create a "last stop." The last stop is an opaque bag or box that will serve as a way station for the stuff you're not ready to release. When the last stop is full, close it up, label it LAST STOP, and date it one year from now. Then stow it in a forgotten corner of your garage or basement. As you move on with your life and you find you need or want an item in the last stop, you can always retrieve it. But you probably won't. In fact, you'll probably forget all about the last stop. A year from now, you'll be able to donate it with ease.

One caveat: the last stop can turn into a pit of indecision, so we challenge you to ONLY use the last stop for a very few items. But this method acknowledges the difficulty of getting rid of emotionally charged stuff, and it gives you the chance to gain some distance while maintaining your progress.

Finding Your Stuff a New Home

It can be tough to start decluttering, but once you get going, it's hard to stop. However, it does create an ironic bottleneck: if you don't have a clear strategy for getting the stuff out the door, your growing pile of newly decluttered stuff creates its own clutter problem. Also, if your kids are like ours, they get curious (and even nervous) about the contents of donation bags and want to rifle through them, which inevitably ends in frustration and tears (either theirs or yours).

Our best advice? Choose the method of distribution that involves the least amount of time and mental overhead. If you enjoy yard sales or selling stuff online, great, but if you don't, consider the few hundred dollars you would have made as an investment in your mental health and *give the stuff away*. Donate it, give it to friends and family, whatever. The good you'll do the universe and yourself will radiate for years to come.

Here's a roundup of ways to move your stuff out the door:

Donate It

In addition to places like Goodwill and the Salvation Army, several charitable organizations will show up at your house with a truck to take away your large donations (even your old car can net you a charitable tax deduction).

Consign It

More and more consignment shops and specialty sale events (particularly for kids' items) are cropping up as parents see the need and utility of recycling. Extra bonus: when you bring in outgrown clothing to consign, you can search for bargains in the next sizes up for your kids.

Sell It Online

This is easier if you're tech savvy, and we recommend it for higher-value items (i.e., the stuff that's worth the effort of listing, communicating with buyers, and shipping). Craigslist and eBay are popular options.

Have a Yard Sale

If tech isn't your thing, try a yard sale. This is more of a logistical time sink (making signs, hauling out goods, etc.) but you get the added bonus of getting to know people in your neighborhood, and your kids will have a ball. Offer a range of interesting items and price things to move (the ultimate goal is to not drag anything back into the house). Another good option is to coordinate a street-wide yard sale with neighbors to entice a bigger crowd. Bonus points if you pass along any remaining items by arranging a donation pickup or by dropping items off at Goodwill directly after the sale.

Our trick with yard sales is to distract the kids so they don't rediscover toys and household items we agreed to pass along. I encourage them to set up a lemonade stand or a separate sale table with a selection of their own stuff. They get to make a little money and exercise their negotiation skills, and we sidestep the temptation to "readopt" old toys.

Swap It

Swapping is another great option, whether you do it with friends or online. In some towns, parents coordinate local e-mail lists and community boards and regularly swap goods and services with other members of the group.

Curb It

Sometimes decluttering/recycling is as easy as leaving things on the curb. One option is to use Freecycle.org, a service that allows you to list items you want to give away; individuals come and pick them up from the curb. Christine lives in an urban neighborhood and she has had good luck simply putting stuff on the curb with a FREE! sign on it. Typically items are gone within the hour; one time a rug she was walking out to the curb didn't even touch the sidewalk. Someone driving by stopped their car, asked if they could take the rug, and off it went with a happy new owner.

Dump It

As a last resort, you can send whatever you can't sell or give away to the dump. For a fee, you can hire a junk disposal company to come to your house, load your stuff in a truck, and haul it away to be disposed of properly. Or, you can take your items to your town dump (be sure to check with your city for proper disposal guidelines).

 One of my girlfriends lives in an affluent Boston suburb where there is no trash pickup; you have to take everything to the town dump on your own. At first I thought, "Man, that's inconvenient. I'd hate to have to schlep my stinky trash to the dump!" But my friend shared two upsides: first, because you have to haul it, you try to proactively reduce waste via recycling or by consuming less. And second, my friend's town dump has turned into a vibrant swapping marketplace via a separate area for hand-me-downs.

Pause to Appreciate the Reward of a Hard Job Well Done

A crucial step in every accomplishment, and one we often forget as parents, is to *stop, acknowledge, and celebrate.* You just did something amazing! Step back and appreciate your hard work. If necessary, grab your partner (or your entire family!) and say, "See what I did? Isn't it great? I'm so proud of myself!" Gloat if you must! Never miss a chance to acknowledge an accomplishment, even if it means patting your own back.

Tidying Up What's Left

Now that you've gotten rid of the clutter, it's time to organize what's left. You might be surprised by how much easier this will be given your newfound space and minimalizing momentum!

If you have an organizing routine in mind, you won't have to rethink it each time you have a few minutes to spend on the job. When it comes to organization, one size does not necessarily fit all. One of our favorite organizing mavens, Meagan Francis of TheHappiestMom.com, shared this wise advice: "The key to getting organized isn't finding that one true perfect system. It's creating a system. *Any* system. And then doing it!"

Here are our best tips for organizing your home quickly and without a lot of fuss. If you need more detailed instructions for top-to-bottom home organization, we list some of our favorite books and resources at the end of this book.

Divide Spaces into Zones Based on Function

As you go through your home, think in terms of what needs to happen in each room or space. Reading, playing, working, conversing, cooking, cleaning, sleeping…you get the picture. By narrowing the function of each space, you can more easily decide what needs to be there.

La Reveuse of thedreamersandme.blogspot.com, via the Minimalist Parenting blog: We've set up zones in the hall closet. My coats are on the left, kids' in the middle, husband's on the right. We put three bins at the top, marked "mittens/gloves," "hats," and "scarves." This makes it so much easier to keep the closet neat, and we can always find what we need!

Triage Incoming Items Immediately

Deal with mail, school papers, and other items as they come into your home: get rid of the unnecessary stuff immediately, put the rest away (instead of setting it aside to deal with later) and shoehorn dates and tasks into your calendar and to-do list.

Group Similar Items in Containers

Files, baskets, boxes, and bins are your friends; ideally, they'll be of complementary size, shape, and color so you can reduce the visual clutter in addition to organizing your stuff. Everywhere in your house, collect similar items into groups and contain them.

Meg via the Minimalist Parenting blog: Save the big sturdy diaper boxes with sizes printed on them and use them to collect clothes your baby has outgrown. They'll automatically be sorted and labeled by size for the next kid.

Paige Lewin of MudroomBoston.com, via BostonMamas.com: We use IKEA shelving with a combination of plastic beverage tubs (to hold chunky toys like bristle blocks and train tracks), plastic lidded boxes (to hold toys that have smaller pieces like LEGO and Playmobil), and built-in rattan baskets for puzzles, games, and dress-up clothes.

Once you've selected your storage system, explain where everything lives to your child (if he or she is old enough)—this will go a long way in both playing and cleaning up.

Label Everything

On the list of gadgets we consider worth buying: a hand-held label maker. Handwritten labels are fine, too, but a label maker somehow adds intention and polish to the whole process. Plus, your kids will be dying to get their hands on it, and will therefore be more than happy to help you make the labels.

Paige Lewin of MudroomBoston.com, via BostonMamas.com: If you have the time and inclination, take pictures of the contents of each toy storage container, then laminate and affix them as labels for pre-readers (even better, include the word and the picture).

Use Short Time Windows to Do Small Jobs

Take advantage of bits of time during the day to tidy up small, manageable areas (Christine likes to do this while waiting for her stove-top espresso to brew). Involve your family in general maintenance throughout the day as well, so cleanup at end of the day won't feel as onerous. Following are examples of tasks you can accomplish in just a few minutes here or there.

Entry

- Stow shoes (in closet or storage bins)
- Hang coats in closet
- Sort mail, recycle junk mail and catalogs, and make a separate stack for items that need tending (e.g., bills)
- Take a load of donations to the car

Kitchen

- Load or empty the dishwasher
- Stow pots/pans/appliances sitting on stove top or countertops

- Clean questionable items out of the fridge
- Sweep the floor
- Empty the trash and recycling

Living Room/Playroom
- Sweep toys into bins
- Stow remotes (in a drawer or storage ottoman)
- Fold throws and put pillows back in place
- Shelve books

Dining Room
- Push all the chairs in
- Clear the table of projects

Office
- Organize paperwork and other materials into to-do piles or files
- Put supplies into bins, cups, or drawers

Bedrooms
- Make beds
- Put away random clothes strewn around
- Tidy the nightstand
- Empty the hamper

Bathrooms
- Neatly fold the hanging towels
- Place all personal care items on a tray
- Clear counters of random odds and ends
- Close the shower curtain and hang the bathmat on the tub
- Stash a couple of extra rolls of toilet paper

 Braden via the Minimalist Parenting blog: Clean out the stroller! We live in New York City, so the stroller is like my car, and you know how dirty and cluttered the backseat of your car gets with kids! The stroller gets the same way for city dwellers.

Taming Paper and Digital Clutter

Paper and digital clutter can be just as draining as the physical clutter around your house. Here are our tips for handling all the information coming into (and hopefully going out of) your home.

Mail, Bills, and Other Paper

There are as many strategies for handling household paper as there are pieces of junk mail strewn across your desk. Here are our best tips for processing the mail (for further reading, check the resources section):

Create a Daily Mail Routine

Do a quick sort-and-toss every time you retrieve the mail. Open and recycle envelopes, along with useless inserts, junk mail, and flyers; place bills to be paid in a labeled basket or file, and put mail that requires follow-up in a second basket or file.

Schedule Regular Time to Handle Action Items

Attend to bills and other such obligations daily or weekly—whatever works for you, as long as it's consistent.

Reduce the Inflow

Sign up for online billing, cancel all but your favorite subscriptions, and register at CatalogChoice.org to reduce junk mail.

Keep As Little Paper As Possible

Unless it's a tax record, legal paper, unpaid bill, or some other official notice, chances are you can shred or recycle it. Before you file anything, think about whether you can get the same information online or via a phone call.

Consider Delegating the Job

If you have an allergy to handling the mail, consider sharing the job with (or passing it on to) your partner.

Kids' Schoolwork and Art

Kids produce *a lot* of paper: some at school in the form of notices, assignments, and projects, some at home in the form of art and writing projects. And while some of it is save-worthy, much of it certainly is not. Here are a few tips on how to manage the flow.

Sort

As with any incoming potential clutter, the first step is to sort the important stuff from the recyclables.

When I walk in with the mail or Laurel hands me a school folder full of papers, I immediately pitch the unnecessary papers in the recycling bin and mark important dates in my calendar (then recycle the notices). It's a small act, but it helps prevent kitchen counter clutter.

Christy via the Minimalist Parenting blog: I have three clipboards—one for each of my children—that hang in our kitchen. Homework assignments, notes from school, birthday party invitations, sports practice schedules, etc., all go on the clipboard. The clipboards can hold a fair amount of paper, but are still limiting, forcing me to declutter regularly.

Contain

Place a basket or file in the entryway or kitchen for all incoming school papers. Allocate one labeled storage box per grade for memorable art/papers; when space is limited, it will force you to trim down and only save what you really want to save.

Display

Kids love to see the products of their creative work displayed for all to admire. Encourage their creativity (and speed along the decluttering) by making room to display and memorialize your kids' work.

Christy via the Minimalist Parenting blog: I bought a ton of wall-safe sticky tabs and we have a rotating art gallery in the hall. They are nice because they hold all sizes and shapes of things, since my elementary schoolers often come home with oddly shaped or large artistic creations.

Another space-friendly method is to create a digital archive by taking photos of kids' most treasured items and collecting them into an album or photo book each year.

E-Mail

E-mail overload is getting to be universal. Christine developed an effective "three-touch rule" to cope with the thousands of e-mails she receives each week. The system helped her come to terms with the reality that it's not only impossible to respond to every query, but that it's perfectly okay to not respond to everything, particularly when lack of response is due to lack of interest.

• **First touch—the first pass.** Open your e-mail and quickly delete and file "easy" e-mails. For example, Christine deletes e-mails that aren't addressed to her personally, files e-mails that are addressed to her but aren't of interest, and responds immediately to time-sensitive matters and work ideas/opportunities/general e-mails that make her happy.

• **Second touch—hitting the ball back.** Respond to e-mails that require more time and energy in order to move things forward (e.g., design or draft something, bullet ideas, create a plan).

• **Third touch—getting rid of the baggage.** This is the final stop for e-mails, and Christine refers to it as the "baggage zone." These e-mails often represent things we don't want to address, don't interest us, or just flat out bug us, but we let them sit there anyway. Get rid of this digital/emotional clutter! Christine figures that if she has touched an e-mail three times and still hasn't responded, she never will. Better to boot the e-mail out of her inbox than let it sit there, encroaching on her productivity.

This method really works! At the time of this writing, Christine has her inbox down to twenty-one messages!

Photos and Videos

Asha remembers loving her first digital camera so much because it meant no more piles of neglected photographs she couldn't seem to organize or bring herself to toss. But digital photos and videos create their own kind of clutter simply because they're so easy to create and save. Here are a few tips on how to keep things under control.

Be a Tough Editor

Christine has become a ruthless photo editor; she values quality over quantity. She strives for small, tightly curated collections of photos. She deletes duplicates and "uglies" (e.g., anyone with eyes half closed, mouth open and full of food, etc.), and photos that are "meh" and don't tell a story.

Develop a Download and Edit System

Get in a habit of downloading then editing/filing/backing up your photos/videos. If you do it in small batches, the process will be less overwhelming. If need be, set up a recurring to-do list item to handle photos.

Digitally Declutter in Small Chunks

If you've got a big digital backlog in need of decluttering, don't fret. Simply address it in small chunks of time. Consider spending ten minutes every few days to edit then arrange remaining photos into digital collections or albums (most photo software contains this feature), and then back everything up onto a separate hard drive or online service.

Added bonus: once you've decluttered your photo collections, photo projects (e.g., albums, calendars, photo books) for holidays and special occasions come together incredibly quickly.

Maintaining Your Minimalized Home

Once your home has been minimalized, maintaining its blissfully decluttered and organized state is easy *as long as* you attend to it regularly. You've already done the hard part; now go the last bit of the distance and build maintenance into your mind-set and practice.

Embrace Your New Role As Curator

As you consider what to let back into your home, remember that you're now a curator of special things—keep this in mind as you consider purchases. It's okay to stumble around a bit here. As long as you buy things you can return (and you keep your receipts), you can change your mind later. Ultimately, your goal is to make smart decisions at the store so that returns are moot.

Nutella via the Minimalist Parenting blog: Keeping my house free of new purchases is the best way to keep it free from clutter. This is made easier by not getting catalogs and by sending e-mail advertisements into a "shopping folder" on my computer (in case I *do* want to buy something, I can access the folder and sale code)! I place items on our wish list, and check it for relevance before birthdays and holidays. It's amazing how something that was a must-have turns into a why-bother with the passage of a little time!

Take decluttering to another level by adhering to the in/out rule: for every item that comes into the house, one goes out.

Follow a Daily Routine

A little daily cleanup makes all the difference, even if it's just ten minutes in the evening. Everyone can pitch in (read on for our tips to make that happen). When you find yourself wanting to slump into bed, too tired to clean up, remind yourself that waking up to a tidy home is an investment in your daily happiness and energy level. Think of it as a gift you're giving *yourself.*

"Outsource" the Stuff

Keep the basics at home (e.g., art supplies, open-ended toys) and let play gyms, art studios, or your local library house the rest. Plan playdate swaps so your kids and their friends can play with different toys at each other's homes.

Getting Others Involved

Finding a place for everything and keeping everything in its place takes time and energy. It warrants closing this chapter with a reminder to *involve other people in the minimalizing and maintenance of the house.* You do not need to do this alone, nor should you.

Share Tasks with Your Partner

If you have a spouse or partner, communicate about shared tasks instead of taking things on in martyr-like fashion and then letting resentment fester. It's counterproductive to stew about what you feel your partner isn't doing when he or she may not know your expectations

Remember, too, that your partner may have a different approach to the task at hand...and that approach may do the job just as well or be even better than yours.

 I was initially shocked by the effectiveness of Jon's laundry zone strategy. When the laundry is done, he dumps it on the floor (or bed) and first sorts it by person, then folds and distributes. It's so much faster to sort everything and then fold rather than mentally categorize/fold/put away clothing for each person.

Finally, keep in mind that modeling the shared domestic workload will pay dividends with your kids for the years to come. We talk in more detail about sharing work with your partner in chapter 3.

Get Your Kids Involved As Soon As Possible

The earlier kids are part of the home maintenance process, the more competent they will become. For many kids, the control that comes with assisting in decluttering also helps the process work more smoothly (if not more quickly). We get into detail about chores and household responsibility in chapter 3, but here are some great community tips for getting kids involved:

La Reveuse of thedreamersandme.blogspot.com, via the Minimalist Parenting blog: Make a 'Clean Up!' playlist and put it on during quick cleanup with the family (and any friends who are there, too!). We have "I Like to Move It," "Firework," "Beautiful Day," "It's a New Day," and a few other upbeat tunes on our playlist. It usually takes two songs to get my living room back to neat and clean if all the kids are helping, and everyone is dancing and having fun.

Jaden via the Minimalist Parenting blog: I definitely involve my four-year-old daughter in the process of decluttering her room and artwork...Sometimes it's me who struggles on letting go because my daughter wants to get rid of something that I don't want her to get rid of (like a book signed and given to her from a relative). I guess I have to model minimal attachment to things. If she is ready to let go, I should be too.

Braden via the Minimalist Parenting blog: I have a trusty kitchen timer, and I will tell my kids "You have X minutes to tidy up, and then we are going to do Y. Anything not put away where it belongs when the timer rings is going to go away" (or to "clutter jail"). I follow through, which I think is the key.

Swap Organizing Help with a Friend

Decluttering and organizing goes a lot faster if you have an impartial person on the team. If you're struggling with separating from your stuff, swap organizing services with a friend. You'll simplify the decluttering process and get quality time with a friend in the bargain.

Hire a Professional

You may not have the time (or desire) to spend scarce free hours decluttering and cleaning. If you can afford it, hiring a professional organizer or house cleaner is a fantastic investment in your progress toward Minimalist Parenting.

Jon and I both work full time, and while I don't mind tackling decluttering projects, cleaning has always been a thorn in my side. I mean, I can do a good job and don't mind the actual process (except for vacuuming, which I detest), but my free time is at a premium. Put more plainly, if given the choice to scrub toilets or hang out with my family, well, that's a no-brainer.

Jon was reluctant about the idea of a cleaning service. But we finally got to a point where deep cleaning was just not happening, things were getting pretty gross, and one of those online local flash sale deals came along (50 percent off a house cleaning) and I said, "We just have to try this. At least once."

The cleaning people came and transformed our house in two short hours. It was truly a miracle and Jon and I were converted. And, quite frankly, from a financial standpoint, it's better for me to pay the cleaners and instead work/bill those hours. Jon and I compromised, and we do light general cleaning maintenance ourselves and have the cleaners come once a month. Best money ever spent in terms of results + sanity. I also decided to gift my mother (who comes and spends time with the girls every week) with a monthly cleaning and it's probably one of the best gifts I've ever given.

The biggest challenge to minimalizing your stuff is simply getting started. You now know how to jump in, get into a rhythm, stem the incoming flow, and take advantage of short time windows and tangible goals. You are not the sole person responsible for this process—involve your family or outsource the jobs that are the biggest drains on your energy and time. Your mind and home will be so much clearer.

6

Financing Your Minimalist Life

Money seems straightforward enough. It's a numbers game, after all: you either have enough or you don't. Right? In our experience, money—thinking about it, handling it, managing it—is rarely that simple. There's more emotional, cultural, and social expectation and stress tied up with finances than most people realize or are willing to admit. The tendency is to assume that more money would solve most problems when, in actuality, more wealth might make your life more complicated.

I'd like to give that version of complicated a try, you're thinking. We hear you! Who'd turn down an extra zero or two on the bank balance? More money *can* bring more freedom and choice...but only to a point. Once your family's basic needs are covered, having fewer constraints on your spending can lead to an increasingly overcrowded, overwhelming life, which is the problem we're trying to solve.

While less isn't exactly more in the case of money, in this chapter we hope to reframe the conversation about family finances. We aren't financial experts, but we are—like you—living with the realities and complexities of money. We view managing money as a way to bring you closer to the life you want, and as a skill to teach your children. If what you want is more clarity and less clutter, it's worth giving some thought to how you're handling your finances now, and how—once minimalized—you may find that you already have enough money to reach your goals.

"Minimalist" Does Not Mean "Minimal"

We're not going to tell you to stop buying stuff. Nor are we going to tell you to forgo pedicures and lattes. *Minimalist* is not the same as *minimal*.

Conversations about frugality sometimes turn saving money into the end goal. But what are you saving your money *for*? When we stress the importance of knowing yourself and your family, defining your values takes a decidedly literal turn. As you begin to think about your finances, ask yourself: What do I consider valuable?

If this topic rings a bell, it's because it echoes our discussion in chapter 2 about time. Both time and money are limited resources, and spending them wisely is a crucial part of Minimalist Parenting. Because of the interrelated nature of time and money (often, when you have more of one, you have less of the other), the question becomes: How do you find balance? How do you use money as a tool to increase and enrich your time?

Deciding What's Worth Your Money

When you minimalize your finances, the focus shifts from "Do I have enough?" to "What do I care about?" As always, the conversation begins with you and your family—your unique needs, wants, and priorities.

We like buying stuff as much as anyone. Christine adds beauty to her home with art (she likes to support an artist friend who creates beautiful paintings) and to her closet with bold accessories (she otherwise keeps her clothing very simple). Asha's a cheapskate in many ways (which causes its own problems), but she doesn't think twice about splurging on travel or a live performance.

All of this costs money, and plenty of it. But the trick is to know the difference between an *expense* and an *investment*. An expense is a cost, plain and simple, whereas an investment is something that enriches your life, either by freeing up time to do more important things or by allowing you to experience something you consider a priority. What elevates an expense to an investment is *meaning* and *long-term gain*, and this will differ for each family. For example, if your top priority is your family's health, you're going to spend more money and time on grocery shopping, meal planning, cooking, and reading about nutrition.

We throw all of our frugal brain cells at reducing expenses so we can funnel money toward investments. Spending isn't the problem. *Spending on stuff that doesn't matter is.* As you evaluate your finances, try to think of your cash flow in terms of expenses versus investments. Ask yourself the following questions:

Do I Need It?

Need is a shifty character. Do you need an expensive standing mixer? If you don't enjoy baking, the answer would be no. However, for those (like Christine!) who find baking a source of joy and family time, the answer might be yes. It warrants noting that you may need that standing mixer but your spouse may also need a Dremel. Who gets dibs on the discretionary spending? This is where shared conversations about your family's values and priorities will pay off (literally).

As you take a critical look at your needs, beware of the "but everyone is buying this" trap. Keep your eye trained on what *you* consider valuable, not on what the world around you is pressuring you to buy. Is a specialized diaper disposal system functionally necessary? No. Will those videos make your baby smarter? Um, probably not.

 Trent of thesimpledollar.com, via the Minimalist Parenting blog: My approach is to look at everything I spend and ask myself if there's not something I actually want more than that. So, if I'm about to spend $10 on a book, I ask myself if there are things in life that I want more than that book, like owning my own home. Which is really more important to me? In other words, finances come down to values.

Another trap: trying to fill holes left from your own childhood. While there may be satisfaction in buying the luxuries your parents couldn't afford (or didn't value), this habit falls dangerously close to throwing money at a problem that would be better solved with introspection and acceptance. Take a closer look at your needs and open yourself to how much they're colored by "want."

Leslee of cr8zygrrlceramics.etsy.com, via the Minimalist Parenting blog: Teach kids the difference between "want" and "need." Don't just preach it; live it. A family disaster required me to completely reevaluate our spending habits. I may not have bought myself any new clothes or shoes in the last three years, but my kids are happy, well cared for, and know they are loved.

Do I Love It?

We don't think "want" is a four-letter word! We all want things. It's perfectly natural, and it's perfectly okay, as long as you're clear on the difference between wants and needs.

But there's also an important distinction between "want" and "love." Loving something—really, truly loving it—puts a select few items into a special category between "want" and "need." We all need beauty and joy in our lives, and there are certain items and experiences, small and large, that embody such beauty and joy. Perhaps it's your saltcellar collection, which reminds you of your grandparents. Or maybe it's the expensive yarn for your knitting projects. Or a piece of art hanging in the local gallery. When chosen mindfully, items you love are an investment in your life's joy.

Will I Learn from It?

Some purchases will change the course of your life. A college education, a vacation, a bicycle that gets you out of your car and exploring your neighborhood, a pet (a hefty investment in money and time, but, for some, a major life changer). You can't always predict when and where "big stuff" will happen, but check in with your inner bus driver—she'll often send you a zing when you're looking at a potentially life-changing opportunity.

I grew up with a thick book of Michelangelo's artwork sitting on my parents' coffee table. I admit that during my elementary school years, what fascinated me most were the naked men (you have to admit, the *David* is pretty hot). But if I really think about what that book added to my life, it was a desire to travel to Italy. I went on to spend several weeks there in college, and to take a year of Italian lessons. And yes, to visit *David* "in the flesh" at the Galleria dell'Accademia in Florence. We're currently trying to figure out how we can take the kids to Italy.

Will It Positively Impact My Life in Other Ways?

Though in general one of the best money-saving tactics is to reduce your spending, sometimes, investing in something can minimalize life in ways that are more valuable and meaningful.

 For 13 years, Jon and I shared a car. Given that we've always lived in urban areas, it wasn't difficult. It only became a problem when Jon started working at a clinic with an untenable public transit commute. He needed the car most weekdays, but we forged on because I loved being eco-friendly (perhaps a bit smugly so, I regret to admit), and whenever I needed a second set of wheels, I used the car-sharing service Zipcar. Laurel and I walked home from school, which was largely fine, save during the occasional snowstorm or monsoon, and when Violet arrived, we stuck with our little car and it forced us to travel incredibly lightly (good), though it was disappointing when we couldn't bring things that would add joy to our travels (e.g., Jon's guitar). The arrangement was okay, except for the times when I had to juggle Zipcar, Laurel, baby Violet, Laurel's booster seat, Violet's car seat, a stroller, and all of our bags. Or when playdates weren't feasible because we didn't have wheels.

When Violet was about six months old, we found ourselves in a very stressful position. We had hired a sitter instead of sending Violet to day care because it was easier logistically due to our one-car status. At first, things seemed fine, but it soon became clear that we needed to make a (fast) change because of some strange goings-on with our sitter.

Jon and I spent a painful amount of energy trying to resolve the situation, brainstorming different at-home child-care solutions and commuting options. The stress of these basic logistics was compounded by the fact that we needed to fire the sitter and secure a new child-care arrangement immediately.

We finally decided to get over ourselves and buy a second car. I admit that I experienced an internal crisis over this. We would no longer be a one-car family! But really, why was I so attached to that label? We went out, bought a second car (used), and right away many other details clicked into place—new paths emerged and the emotional and logistical clutter began to dissipate. We were able to solve the sitter situation. A spot at Laurel's former day care opened up just at the right time. Jon and I were able to split drop-off duties so we could both get our workdays going on time and with less stress. We were able to transport Laurel and her friends around and become part of a "village" ride sharing solution with other parents for school, soccer, and playdates. We could fit everyone in our eight-seater when my in-laws came to town.

I couldn't believe we hadn't made the decision earlier.

A Minimalist Approach to Money Management

Can you be a responsible steward of your family's money if you don't balance your checkbook or follow a budget? Yes! (That realization alone may be worth the price of this book.) Like other things in life, money management isn't a right/wrong dichotomy but rather a process you create based on where you are right now and what you need going forward.

If you're doing okay financially—there's enough money every month to pay the bills and see a movie or two but not much for savings—you're fine tracking the larger expenses by category and letting go of the details. You'll be able to gain enough data at that level of insight to shift your spending and make progress toward your savings goals. If, on the other hand, you're drowning in credit card debt and living paycheck to paycheck, you'll need to spend more time and attention on budgeting in order to get on top of it. It's fine. You start where you are and go from there. The best method is the one that works with minimum fuss.

Tracking Your Cash Flow

Money in, money out. That's cash flow. Before you can improve your financial circumstances, you need information about where you currently stand. With credit and debit card spending, electronically deposited paychecks, automatic bill pay, and all the rest, it can be surprisingly easy to lose sight of reality where your finances are concerned.

The first step is to track your income and spending for a month or two. Yes, it's a bummer, because you want to jump in and fix the problem RIGHT NOW. But tracking your cash flow will show you where the problems are. Perhaps the problem is too much money spent on takeout. Or cell phone plans. Or groceries. Perhaps you're a freelancer with multiple sources of income, and one of your jobs doesn't pay nearly as much per hour as the others. How will you know unless you have ballpark dollar amounts you're earning and spending?

If all you need is high-level information, you can probably find it by logging in to your bank's online system. Some banks' systems include an expense-tracking feature and, because all of your data is already there, it shouldn't be difficult to figure out.

 Cynth via the Minimalist Parenting blog: For those who can't deal with a lot of data, I have a REALLY simple spreadsheet: I just track the money in and money out of each checking account each month. I get the data when the account statements come (since I have to reconcile my checkbook anyway) and put it in literally once a month for all of the sixty seconds it takes. Then I can tell whether we're on track to cover spending with revenues or whether we need to make adjustments later in the year.

If you need more detailed information, you can do it manually by categorizing and entering daily receipts, or you can sign up for a service such as Mint.com or Adaptu.com. Both pull data directly from your bank to spare you tiresome data entry.

Most importantly, you need to find the level of detail that makes *you* feel most comfortable.

Kelly Whalen of thecentsiblelife.com, via the Minimalist Parenting blog: It's called *personal finance* for a reason. I think the key to stressing less about money is having a cushion in place, and living well within your means.

While automating expenses, bill paying, and savings works for some people, others (myself included) prefer to be more hands on. Spending an hour or so a week focusing on our money actually keeps me tuned in to how much we are spending.

Finally, it's worth acknowledging the guilt and anxiety you may feel as your financial picture comes into focus. *How did we let our finances get to this point? How will we afford to send our kids to college, let alone retire? How will we ever be able to save up an emergency fund?* These are all reasonable questions with specific answers. Rather than worrying about leaping the chasm between where you are now and where you want to be, try instead to focus on how brave you are for taking the first step (YAY YOU), and what your next step is going to be. You're making progress! That's what matters.

Building Your Financial Foundation

Once you've got a decent view of your overall financial picture, you're ready to adjust your spending so you can build a plan. These are your long-term priorities for a strong financial foundation.

Save for an Emergency

Work toward putting three- to six-months-worth of living expenses in an emergency savings account. We're talking basic living expenses: mortgage or rent, food, utilities, the necessities. This protects you in case something big knocks you off your income-earning feet for a few months.

Save for Retirement

Once you've got an emergency fund set aside, start with whatever monthly retirement savings amount seems doable, and then try to increase it each month. The key point to keep in mind: the more you save *sooner*, the less you'll have to save *overall*. Compound interest is your friend. Try not to worry about whether it's "enough" for now. Just get started.

Save for College

Yep, retirement first, then college. Because no one's giving you a scholarship to retire.

There are other pieces (e.g., insurance, estate planning) you need as part of a complete financial plan, but why overwhelm yourself right out of the gate? No matter what, this is a great place to start. If you want to explore personal finance further, we share some great resources at the end of this book.

Reducing Your Spending

It's obvious that spending less will help you save more. But it can be difficult to figure out where to begin, particularly if you're already living lean. The answer lies in what we discussed earlier in the chapter: being clear about what you consider valuable.

Remember the More and Less List you drew up in chapter 2 to shed light on how you want to spend your time? Apply this same list to money. Look at the data you uncovered during your cash flow tracking and see if you can find where you're spending on things you don't really care about. The specifics will be unique to you, but here are some common culprits:

- High-end items, such as a house that's bigger than you need or car payments/insurance when you don't really use that extra car
- Premium TV channels, when you barely watch TV
- Long-distance phone service, when you use your cell phone most of the time
- Takeout, when a little bit of attention to meal planning would solve dinnertime dilemmas (see chapter 11 for inspiration)
- Expensive weekend entertainment, when a bike ride, board game, or a free concert in the park would be just as fun
- Big-ticket travel, when a creative staycation could provide ample adventure

Karen of moneysavingenthusiast.com, via the Minimalist Parenting blog: When it comes to being a minimalist parent on a budget, my philosophy is "What would a mom in the '70s or '80s do?" I think of all of the things I did as a kid. I try to raise my kids with good old-fashioned fun. We play Wiffle ball, throw footballs, and watch movies at home. We splurge on special occasions and go to baseball games when we have the money. When you pick your priorities and set your budget, you learn how to be creative.

Keep in mind one of the keys of Minimalist Parenting: *course correction beats perfection*. Make one or two changes to your spending, see how they feel, then make a few more. Reducing your spending can be surprisingly painless when you approach it gradually, with a spirit of experimentation and willingness. It's empowering to discover that a full, fun life can be had for much less money than you thought.

Increasing Your Income

The other piece of the savings equation is income. If more money is coming in, that's as good as saving, right? Well, yes, *as long as you don't spend it all*. Bigger paychecks have a way of super-sizing "needs," just as bigger houses tend to fill with more clutter.

The other tricky part about making more money: you'll have to cut into your available time to do it. Before you commit to a job (or a second job), check with your partner and your inner bus driver to see if that's a sacrifice you're willing to make. On the other hand, outside work may be just what you need. If, for example, you're craving adult interaction and recognition in the outside world, paid work could do wonders for much more than the bottom line.

If you and your family decide that more income is the way to go, and you commit yourself to throwing most of the money you make into your savings, more power to you! Are there some smart investments you can make to exchange money for time? Perhaps a house-cleaner would free up enough hours for you to not only pay for the help but to invest in yourself even further.

As for the how-to for making more money, Christine recommends two reflective angles on the process:

Since leaving academia to forge a freelance career, there are two perspectives I have adhered to that have proven immensely beneficial. The first is to *set intentions* about what you are trying to achieve. Perhaps it sounds a little woo woo, but Jon and I believe strongly in the power of setting intentions (a first cousin of your inner bus driver). It's incredibly powerful to be specific about how you want your life to shape up. Now, this is not genie in a bottle kind of stuff—saying, "I want to win the lottery tomorrow!" is not going to cut it. Instead, setting intentions involves examining your life, seeing what you have in front of you, and deciding what may be within your reach, and what you deserve/want to make happen.

Intentions don't always revolve around money, but one year I looked at my skills and the palette of work I was doing and said, "I'm doing pretty well but I really think I deserve to be earning [insert large income jump]." I set this intention, started to plant some seeds to move in this direction, and by the next year, I was where I wanted to be.

The second perspective involves a mantra I picked up from Jon: *opportunities can be dangerous.* When you're eager to get ahead, it's tempting to leap at every opportunity that comes your way. Before you jump, gauge your initial reaction (happy, cringing, disappointed, etc.) and evaluate the time/money tradeoff. If your inner bus driver tells you to step hard on the brakes and say no to that opportunity, listen to her. This won't be your last opportunity. Hold out for something that will bring both money *and* joy.

Simplifying Your Financial Setup

Another place to minimalize your finances is in the infrastructure: the bank accounts, savings accounts, credit cards, and bill paying and how they all work together. The less time you spend tinkering with the mechanics of your financial system, the less it will feel like a chore, and the more it will work for you.

It's easier to keep track of the daily spending when there are fewer moving parts. Some families pay nondiscretionary bills (mortgage, insurance, etc.) with the checking account while confining discretionary spending to a single credit card. One of our blog readers came up with this simple and low-tech solution:

Jessica of thedebtprincess.com, via the Minimalist Parenting blog: On the first of the month, I pull out the cash and place it into each envelope for the month. I don't even carry my debit card with me, just my envelopes in an organizer. This way I am guaranteed to stay within my VERY SMALL budget.

If the idea of carrying around that much cash seems inconvenient, a clever *Parent Hacks* reader modified the system by using gift cards.

Automating Spending, Saving, and Bill Paying

There are two trains of thought when it comes to automating your finances. The first says that the less you think about it, the more you're likely to follow through with your savings plans. The second says that autopilot = taking your eye off the ball, which is part of the problem.

Only you can decide whether automation will help or hinder your progress toward your financial goals. We're fans of automation simply because it frees brain cells for other pursuits. Convert paper paychecks to direct deposit. Familiarize yourself with your bank's online banking system to see what kinds of automation you can set up (e.g., bill pay, between-account transfers).

Kim @observacious, via the Minimalist Parenting blog: My mother always told me to "pay yourself first." That's become even easier with the world of direct deposit and automatic transfers. Our money automatically gets [split up and] dispersed into long-term savings (for unspecified purposes), short-term savings (for upcoming expenditures, usually for the house), into "play" accounts for my husband and me, and into our joint checking account. Although I always try to keep some money in the main checking account as a buffer, for the most part we manage the balance. If the balance is already low by midmonth we know we'll need to be a bit more austere in the remaining weeks. Because the account splits happen up front I know that even in months when we push the limits of our checking account we have also managed to save a bit.

 Adrienne of babytoolkit.com, via the Minimalist Parenting blog: We set up a separate account that we think of as an escrow account for big (boring) annual expenses: property taxes, insurance premiums, auto licensing, etc.

Annually, I total the last year's fees and divide by the number of pay periods (twelve for us, because our income is monthly). We direct deposit that amount plus a small cushion to cover rate changes (maybe $150 per year). When the big bills hit, there's no scramble to assemble the funds needed.

Again, start small. If the idea of transfers among multiple accounts makes your head explode, start with a monthly $50 transfer to your savings account. As you get comfortable working with your money, you'll quickly find more ways to save time and effort.

Hiring Professional Help

You appreciate the minimalist mantra, but the whole money thing still freaks you out. If so, hiring financial help (an accountant, financial planner, bookkeeper, etc.) may be a good investment in your financial *and* mental health.

Let us reassure you: the basics of a good personal financial plan are simple and straightforward for anyone to learn. Even a little bit of reading on the topic will give you a leg up on the average consumer (see the resources section at the end of the book for recommendations). A little education is in order even if you do decide to work with a professional, if only to help you ask more intelligent questions. Impartial advice can also help you make the leap from thinking to doing.

Stacie of hometownperch.com, via the Minimalist Parenting blog: My husband and I had tried every approach in the book and we were still living paycheck to paycheck. What works for others just did not work for us. But what did work for us finally was going through Financial Peace University (FPU). We started the class a few months ago and it has honestly changed our lives forever.

Teaching Kids About Money Management

No matter the state of your family finances, you can teach your kids basic money skills and how their dollars can be spent, whether on themselves or others. Here are some ideas for how to get started.

Inbound Money

The first phase of learning about money management involves understanding where money comes from (i.e., not from trees). Whether your kids receive a gift or payment for a job, income is the first step in learning about the mechanics of saving money and prioritizing purchases.

Allowance

You may decide to give your kids an allowance so they can start learning how to manage their money. Your allowance system doesn't need to be complicated; simply decide on a reasonable weekly amount, and be consistent. As for when to begin, we think it makes sense to start during the early elementary years, when math and numbers are a daily topic of conversation—say, when your child is about seven or eight.

As for amounts, it's really up to you and the system you create. One rule of thumb suggests $1 per year of age, but that may be too much if allowance is more of a token payment, or not enough if you expect your kids to take on more buying responsibility.

Rael and I found that we never had enough cash on allowance day, which reduced the effectiveness of the whole exercise. So we started using the mobile app-based "debit" system KiddyBank, which automatically adds a weekly allowance to each kid's ledger. When someone wants to make a purchase, we deduct the price from his or her total spending money. The beauty of this system: everyone knows how much spending money is available.

Payment for Chores

Chores teach kids how to build everyday skills and function as part of a household, and also help reduce your load. Though some families believe that kids should not receive payment for chores, others use payment as a way to motivate kids to get chores done and learn about the work-for-money exchange. It's also worth noting that there's a meeting ground between the two approaches.

My siblings and I worked hard when we were kids. Very hard. We worked both around the house and at my parents' market, where we all put in time after school, during the evenings, and on weekends (I started working in elementary school). We were not paid for any of this work (until much later, when I was in high school), and I don't recall any of us grousing about it. It was just part of our family system and livelihood.

Consequently, I am one of those parents who bristles at the thought of paying for chores that reflect everyday helping activities. That said, I realize that Laurel is an accommodating and helpful kid—we don't have to coerce her to help, which is a common reason payment gets hinged to chores.

Last year Jon and I came upon a middle ground. We give Laurel a weekly allowance ($3) which she can use to experiment with saving and spending. Everyday helping chores (e.g., laundry, tidying up) are expected and not hinged to payment. However, if an unusual, more involved job comes up and we feel the situation warrants, we'll offer a small payment and it's up to her whether she wants to take us up on it.

And the funny thing? Sometimes Laurel turns down the payment or offers to do it for less. One time we offered her a couple of dollars to help us wash the car and afterwards, she said, "You know, Mom, how about just one dollar? Because that was a pretty fun job for me, too."

Gifts

At some point, your child will start receiving cash gifts. Whatever the bill size, it's probably going to be a big deal when your child receives a lump sum, and it will provide a good opportunity to talk about saving and spending.

Paid Work

Kids gain skills and self-esteem from doing real, useful, challenging work. As they get older, there will be more and more options for what they can do. Encourage them on the journey; you'll be amazed by what they learn.

 I still vividly remember the day I talked to my mom on the phone from my freshman dorm room and she told me that she and my dad could no longer provide financial support for college. The call was not mean spirited; it was purely pragmatic given that I was the sixth child to go through college. As we ended our my mom said, "Anyway, Christine, we're not worried about you. You always find a way to make things happen."

And though I don't wish that level of stress on anyone (I did some serious ugly crying at my college's financial aid office), it is 100 percent true that this situation helped me develop the work ethic and confidence that is the cornerstone of everything I do today. I learned about time management and budgeting. I learned how to find jobs and operate in professional environments. I learned that you could pretty much learn any work skill on the fly if you needed to. I learned that you can push yourself to work incredibly hard if the result is meaningful to you (every summer I worked an office job during the day then took the bus to my evening job at a local ice cream store...yes, it was exhausting). During college, I never missed a class unless I was deathly ill because the privilege of sitting in those classes was directly linked to my long summer working hours.

Perhaps most important of all, I grew a new appreciation for my parents and their struggles around money. One day my mom called me in tears, after having opened an envelope from me, asking me why I was sending her money. It turned out that between my summer and winter breaks, I earned enough to pay my tuition not covered by financial aid. I knew she and my dad were still struggling so it made sense to me to send these checks home. In retrospect, they were such small, piddly checks (I think I earned something like $4.65 an hour at the college library) but I suspect it felt like a million bucks to my mom.

With time, your kids' money pile will grow and at some point you will want to shift from "under the mattress" to a bank. Christine found that Laurel felt so excited and grown up when she and Jon opened her bank account. It's a big day when a child realizes that her savings officially have a home.

Outbound Money

On the other side of the money spectrum is spending. As you know, we are big advocates of spending wisely on things that matter. And the good news is that, as you work toward this goal, it will be easier to help your kids get there, too. The approach to kids' spending is simple: they will think longer and harder about whether or not to spend if they are the ones who have to pay for it.

My kids spend their own money on anything that isn't a necessity or a gift (extra clothes, video games, toys, etc.). As such, their allowance is high enough to put saving for a $40 item into a reasonable time frame. When the kids are in complete control of their spending money, they learn much more about budgeting and assigning value.

One area where my practical upbringing wouldn't budge—overcompensation issues be damned—was American Girl (AG) dolls. When Laurel asked for one, I told her I simply would not spend $105 on a doll. We were close to Christmas, though, so I suggested that if my family asked about a wish list, she could ask for small (e.g., $5-10) contributions to a doll fund.

At Christmas, Laurel received almost the entire amount for a doll in cash gifts. She put in $10 of her own money and Jon and I chipped in the tax (generous, I know). Jon also offered to take Laurel to the store, which I thought was probably worth $500 of parent-sanity currency, given that I'd directed him to the wrong shopping mall and the correct mall was forty-five minutes away (never mind that a doll store is probably the last place Jon would want to spend an afternoon). They persevered and purchased the doll, and Laurel has played with it an impressive amount. I think part of this had to do with having thought so long and hard about the acquisition, having directed all of her Christmas requests to this one item, and having contributed to buying it.

Now, one might think the story ends here, but a month after Christmas, Laurel received a late gift—a generous $50 gift certificate to the AG store. Laurel perused the AG website and decided that she wanted another doll (for playdate purposes). I groaned a little. Okay, a lot. We told Laurel that if she wanted to buy another doll, she would need to pay the entire difference plus tax and shipping (because neither Jon nor I were willing to go to the store, even though we knew where it was this time around). She looked troubled, as withdrawing $70 to $80 from her bank account was clearly not something she wanted to do. I suggested selling some of her high-value, rarely used toys and that since I was always happy to get unused things out of the house, I would help her list items on Craigslist.

Laurel proceeded to pick items from her toy collection to sell, we listed them, I managed the e-mails and appointments, and within a couple of days she had enough money to pay for the balance, tax, and shipping for her second AG doll. I helped her order online and she was proud of the purchase and even had some money left over to put into her savings.

After I closed my laptop I figured we were done with the AG conversation. And then I felt a tug on my sleeve. Laurel had one more question: "Mom, you really should get something for helping me sell those toys and order the doll. Does an ice cream + $5 seem like a fair payment?" I couldn't stop smiling.

Charitable Giving

Finally, charitable giving is worth mentioning, as it teaches your kids about the wider world. If including a charitable component in your kids' financial setup feels overwhelming at first, feel free to hold off for now. But, for many families, charitable giving completes the spending/saving picture by showing kids that their money can make a difference in the world.

After learning about rainforest endangerment at school, Laurel kicked off a summer-long rainforest fund-raising drive via lemonade stands, puppet shows, and jewelry sales.

You also can frame conversations about charitable giving with your kids through general family gifts.

My Kids' Mom of pookandbug.blogspot.com, via the Minimalist Parenting blog: My husband and I get requests for money from charities almost every day. We set up a monthly budget for charity. Each year we choose eleven charities. We try to choose a variety that reflect our values and are diverse so we don't load up one type, such as all environmental. Then, each month we send the same amount of money out as a donation. Each charity gets one month, our budget stays even, and we have a simple answer to get off the phone ("Sorry, we didn't choose you this year, but we will consider your cause next year"). You may notice that we only give to eleven charities in a twelve-month year. We know that friends, family, and coworkers will come up with something and the final open month gives us the chance to be more spontaneous.

Money typically is a topic that inspires anxiety and dread. But you're now taking the steps to decide what's worth your spending, gather data, and work out systems and practices that work for *you*. Yes, it takes an investment in time to wade through the emotional and practical budgetary details, but once you get to the other side, you'll unlock energy (and possibly more money) for the important things in your life.

SIX WAYS TO SAVE HUNDREDS A YEAR

Saving money can be easier—and sometimes more fun—than you think. We asked the ever-stylish bargain hunter Melissa Massello, "Stealfinder in Chief" at Shoestring Magazine (shoestringmag.com), to share some of her favorite, most innovative ways to save money:

DIY versus Buy

Instead of running around town to various stores, burning gas and precious time in search of the best deal, consider making favorite staples (whatever those might be for your family) from scratch. DIY projects such as homemade play dough or granola are a great way to get kids and parents working together, learning new skills, spending quality time together, and contributing to family needs, providing a sense of accomplishment and lasting memories/habits that kids will (hopefully) take into adulthood. And not only can DIY save you money, it allows you to control what goes into the things your family consumes—keeping toxic or questionable ingredients out of your home (and growing bodies). Pinterest was made for finding countless DIY ideas for anything you might like to try from scratch.

Marble Jar Money Lessons

My best friend from childhood now has three beautiful kids (ages three, five, and eight), and she and her husband have made certain things like consuming fresh, organic fruits and vegetables a priority for their family—and their budget. Each time their kids ask to go out for a meal, they ask the kids what they would order. If, for example, it's chicken, broccoli, and ziti, they note that there's chicken, broccoli, and ziti already in the fridge, and ask whether they'd *really* like to use that money for a meal out or if they'd rather save it for something fun, like going out for ice cream or to the movies. Each time the kids make the savings decision, a colorful marble goes into a mason jar on the kitchen windowsill. When the jar is full, they do something really fun as a family, whether it's something inexpensive like a picnic followed by a trip to the local ice cream store or something a little more splurge-y such as a Red Sox game. The kids quickly learned about the benefits of saving for something special.

Move It to Savings

For adults, it's one thing to say that we're "saving" by not spending, but when that money is just sitting in our checking accounts it's A) likely to just be spent on something later and B) not gaining valuable interest. Any time you employ savings tactics like DIY-ing something from scratch or saving with your kids through the marble jar method, use a tool like ImpulseSave or SmartyPig to quickly and efficiently estimate the amount you saved and actually *move that money into your savings account*, where it will grow in value. During a two-month experiment, I saved $259.90 plus forty-five cents in interest, without even really trying. This. Works.

Meal Planning and Food Priorities

In September of 2008, two San Diego public school teachers named Christopher Greenslate and Kerri Leonard decided to try an experiment: Could they each live on just $1 per day for food, the global average? (They subsequently attempted to each live on $4.13 per day, or $462 per month, the food stamp allotment for a family of four in the United States.) Their resulting blog-to-book, *On a Dollar a Day,* is a must-read for anyone trying to budget, and also brings up dozens of food source and food justice issues for families to consider and learn from. The number one takeaway: by simply prioritizing ingredients, buying in bulk, and planning each week's meals in advance, families can save hundreds of dollars per month on food alone.

Budgets Are Sexy

Make budgeting a fun weekly activity by motivating yourself, your partner, or your family with a small indulgence after the budget has been updated each week, like a make-your-own ice cream sundae bar (or a post-dinner glass of a favorite wine for the adults) and a recent-release movie On Demand at home.

Sunday nights are generally the best time to do the weekly budget, because everyone is preparing for the week and is more likely to remember upcoming expenses like field trips, club/team dues, classes, birthdays, and so on. "J. Money" of the aptly named blog budgetsaresexy.com has collected hundreds of tools, tips, and resources to help you get started and stay on budget while having a laugh, if not a blast.

Embrace Secondhand Style

Between the states of the economy and the environment, buying secondhand really has become part of many peoples' everyday lives. As cofounder of The Swapaholics, I've gotten to participate in the "collaborative consumption" movement—also known as good, old-fashioned sharing and common-sense resourcefulness. By borrowing, renting, sharing, swapping, and thrifting the things we need for the time we need them—versus owning them forever—families can save thousands of dollars per year. Tech startups like Netflix (movies) and Zipcar (transportation) paved the way for a worldwide sharing movement that now includes everything from renting houses (Airbnb) to cocktail dresses (Rent the Runway). Swapping clothes, kids' gear, sporting goods, books, games, even food, through swap events like ours or those held by organizations like Peace, Love, Swap, or through websites like swapmamas.com will help families turn what they already own into what they need and save thousands of dollars per year in the process. There's a swapping or sharing community for practically anything you might need, from power tools to hockey goals. Plus, often the items you find at swaps or Goodwill are brand new!

7

Playtime: Good, Simple Fun

P lay is the work of children." A version of that quote is attributed to a number of people including noted educator Maria Montessori, and we couldn't agree more. (We would add that play is just as important for grown-ups.) Everyone needs open, unstructured time to get creative, follow a train of thought, run off energy, and extend his or her imagination beyond the distance of a computer screen or to-do list. We all deserve the freedom of no agenda every now and then.

But we also realize that the prospect of long stretches of empty time (especially with little kids) can be daunting. If left to their own devices, will the kids draw all over the walls? Dig up the backyard? Drive you nuts?

In this chapter, we offer our minimalist take on playtime, both solo and with friends.

You Don't Have to Play with Your Kids All the Time

While you may be your child's primary playmate (especially when she's little), you are *not* obligated to be available every moment of the day. Togetherness, fun, and bonding are some of the greatest gifts of parenting, but you also have a right to grown-up time. The sooner you give your child an opportunity to experience the wonders of independent play, the happier you'll both be.

Some kids are naturally flexible—they toddle around the house hap-pily (if messily) keeping themselves busy. For others, it's a longer-term learning process. Start by keeping interesting toys nearby (say, in the kitchen) and encouraging your child to entertain herself for five min-utes while you cook dinner. Keep talking about it being "her" playtime and "your" cooking time, reinforcing the distinction.

As your kids get older, maintain that distinction, setting the expec-tation that there is time together and time when you need to attend to grown-up business around the house. When you set kind but firm boundaries, your kids will eventually come to accept the implicit understanding that they are responsible for entertaining themselves.

 When Laurel was a baby I felt like I needed to engage her every waking moment, which was not the best for her (from an independence-building standpoint) or me. During my maternity leave, I swear I was more exhausted at the end of the day than on the days when I went to work following my leave. I probably was overcompensating for a childhood with very little parental supervision or recreational engagement (e.g., I cannot recall ever having been read to by my parents). This is no knock on my parents—clearly, I turned out okay—it was just the reality of being the sixth of seven children.

With Violet, it's been so different. Not only am I more laid back and trust that she is getting enriched plenty by everyday life, but there's also the reality that I now have two kids. So, while I log a good deal of time reading books and singing "Wheels on the Bus" and cheering Violet on as she discovers the wonders of the ring stacker, corn popper, and singing teapot, she has also learned to play on her own.

We have a deep bottom drawer in the kitchen where we keep kid-friendly dishes, cups, and lunch containers. This has become one of Violet's favorite places to play while I wash dishes, cook dinner, sort mail, or hungrily flip through *InStyle* when it arrives in the mail. The other day while I was standing at the kitchen counter flipping through said magazine, Violet was—as usual—making a huge mess at my feet, dumping everything out of the drawer. Suddenly, it got quiet and then she started laughing. She had discovered that she could put smaller containers inside of larger containers. I smiled, turned back to my magazine and thought, "Perfect, we're both happy playing."

Fewer Toys Equals More Play

The "fewer toys" mantra goes beyond simply clearing household clutter. With fewer toys to distract them or mire them in the "what should I play with now?" decision spiral, kids often find renewed inspiration for creative play.

We live in a condo with a lovely loft on the third level. Half serves as Jon's man cave and half as guest space/ playroom. I loved this space when we first moved in because it meant I now had a place to deposit all the toys I didn't want to see downstairs.

However, I recently realized that our playroom was tragically wasted real estate. It was messy and cluttered, and every time I went upstairs to think about dealing with it, I felt overwhelmed and went back downstairs. Laurel and her friends would go up, complain that there was nothing to play with (because the mess obscured the toys available), and come back down as well.

Finally, I had had enough. I grabbed two trash bags (one for trash, one for donations) and a paper bag for recycling and was *ruthless*. It was shocking, but within one hour, I had decluttered and organized the playroom. It looked light, bright, and welcoming.

When Jon and Laurel saw the playroom they were both *thrilled*. Violet was also psyched to have a new carpeted space to pad around. I organized the toys so that all of the little chokeables were situated on the large built-in ledge space out of Vi's reach. Everything that was Violet-friendly was contained in different bins (wooden, plastic, soft) on the floor. We set up our card table with a large puzzle for the grown-ups to work on and all of a sudden, the playroom was a fun space for the whole family to enjoy.

Work As Play

We're not suggesting you pull a fast one by spinning kids' chores as playtime. But there's no need to make a big distinction between the two, either. For toddlers and preschoolers especially, household work is fun. Cleaning the table with a washcloth and a small squirt bottle, sweeping the floor, beating cake batter with a hand mixer, spreading cream cheese onto a bagel...many kids love to do real, grown-up work, especially when the inherent fun is pointed out. (For more on chores, see chapter 3.)

 When I was a kid, yard work always seemed onerous because all we did was remove stuff—weeds, leaves, cut grass, etc. But, oh, the joy of *adding*. I am not an experienced gardener by any stretch, but the great thing about gardening projects is that they can be as simple or complex as you want them to be depending on your space, motivation, and need for immediate gratification. Whenever I head out to do yard work (planting flowers, spreading mulch, weeding) and ask Laurel if she wants to join me, she almost always says yes. There's a visceral joy in playing with dirt, but I think part of it is that she just likes being outside together.

 Older kids also love "playing in the dirt," especially when there's money and power equipment involved. Sam stands pretty tall as he's pushing the mower across the front lawn. I rarely need to ask him twice.

What About Electronics?

Electronics are a mixed blessing. They can be wonderful tools, helping your child learn numbers and colors, providing the musical backdrop against which to rock out (Violet spins happily in circles as soon as she hears music), or encouraging a reluctant reader. Handheld games and DVDs can pass the time when you're in transit. Sometimes, they're a convenient way to occupy the kids when you simply need to catch your breath, get through your e-mail, or reconnect with your partner.

 Laurel has expressed interest in dance classes, but the main thing holding her back is the recitals. Unlike me (I love performance and joyfully embraced solo violin recitals), Laurel is not interested in (read: is terrified by the prospect of) being on stage in front of a group of strangers.

One day, when I picked her up from a playdate, Laurel and her friend were panting and laughing hysterically. I asked what was up and they led me to the living room, fired up the Wii, and broke into mimicking the Wii choreography to the song "Apache." It was *totally awesome*. Not only was I impressed by how coordinated they were with the choreography, but I loved seeing Laurel dancing and having such a great time.

Laurel has asked for a Wii a couple of times since then. I don't have a problem buying one per se, but it just hasn't been on the top of my priority list. I told Laurel that a Wii is not a family purchasing priority right now, but that she can put it on her wish list for an upcoming birthday or holiday (and see if it's *her* priority by that point), and otherwise enjoy it with her friend when they have playdates at her house. She was totally fine with that.

The other side of the coin is the electronic vortex: the hours and opportunities for family togetherness that slip away while your child is plugged in. There are also the arguments and negotiations that arise over who gets to control the game system (or iPad or television), for how long, and whether electronics time happens before or after homework. As kids get older, there are issues of mature content in video games, and safety and security via the web and texting.

The key is to find a balance in which electronics become a *tool*, not an obstacle or continuous point of friction. The specifics of how you handle the introduction and control of electronics will be unique to your family. Cultural background, educational philosophy, access, parents' own interests and careers, and temperaments all come into play. For every family in which there's a nine-year-old Xbox addict, there's another with a kid who could care less about video games. Wherever your family happens to be on the electronics spectrum, we recommend communicating that electronics are a privilege and not an assumption, framing some general rules around the use of electronics (e.g., when, how long, what chores need to be done before this privilege is enjoyed), and, when necessary, establishing whether it's a "need versus a want" addition to the array of playtime options.

Erin via the Minimalist Parenting blog: I am a stay-at-home mother and my husband works long hours. We have kids who don't need a lot of sleep, and never have. But one sanity saver for us is Friday nights. My husband makes sure he's home by 6:30 p.m., and I've already fed the kids something easy. While we control media every other day, on Friday nights they are required to stay in their bedrooms with the iPad or Nintendo DS or whatever. My husband and I have a more adult meal (nice takeout, for instance) and then usually watch a DVD together. We call it "date night." Even though we can't afford a babysitter four times a month, this has really helped. Our kids are six and eight now, but we started this tradition when the youngest was three. Otherwise, we're rarely "off-duty" until 10 p.m.

Finally, similar to our approach to sweets in chapter 12, when considering your stance on electronics, keep in mind that moderation is often a better long-term solution than total deprivation. Having open conversations about electronics instead of vilifying them, and setting reasonable and firm limits will likely reduce the friction they can cause.

Being Social

Playtime! It's what kids do! At least it's what they *used* to do. That we're even writing a how-to for playtime says something about the trend toward busy-and-prescribed in modern kids' lives.

But not in *your* minimalist life! As you edit the activity "noise" from your schedule, you'll notice that delicious spans of free hours will materialize during the week. Time for independence, exploration, and friends.

The Art of the Playdate

Playdates are good for kids *and* parents. They offer opportunities for kids to be flexible and figure out how to compromise (because there will invariably be a scuffle about something). Playdates provide a chance for deeper friendships, which are sometimes difficult to forge in the chaos of the school playground, particularly for shy kids. They allow kids to, well, play—to make up complicated, fanciful games parents don't always understand, and to chatter on with peers in ways that parents don't always have the patience for. Finally, playdates offer parents space—while you may be involved in the planning, it doesn't mean you need to be at the center of the playing. The goal is to let the *kids* play, not to act as director of playlike activity.

If you're new to playdate etiquette, here are a few guidelines to help you settle in to your new role as invisible host (or drop-off parent).

Set the Ground Rules

Whether your child is the host or the guest, make it clear that manners matter. Encourage your child to be flexible when it comes to deciding what to do, and remind him that sharing toys and activities makes them more fun. Practice with your child how to state a preference in a friendly, respectful way, and how to compromise if a playmate doesn't agree. If you're hosting, go over the rules once the friend arrives so that everyone hears the same thing at the same time. If you're dropping off, share with the hosts that you've explained the rules to your child. It will invariably work out in the wash that sometimes your kid will start the playdate by doing what the other kid wants, and sometimes he'll get to start with what *he* wants. Good manners will rule, and compromise and flexibility are always worth working toward.

Be a Fly on the Wall

Kid play, at its best, is as much an internal mental activity as it is an external physical one. Your kids may *look* like they're playing with Playmobil, but they're actually plotting the overthrow of an evil alien invasion force. When you show up and get involved, you run the risk of breaking the spell.

Provide a Well-Timed Snack
Up the chances of harmonious play by fueling kids with a healthy snack and a glass of water. No need for fancy, just something satisfying. When her kids were younger, Asha used to break out the snacks when she detected discord. Sometimes the distraction was all it took to get everyone back in sync.

Give Them a Chance to Work It Out
In the face of disagreements, resist the urge to rush in and save the day. Kids need to practice their negotiation skills and learn how to get along with each other. Don't short-circuit the learning by giving everyone the answer too quickly.

End on a Good Note
The old adage "leave them wanting more" applies to playdates. More important than elaborate fun is a happy ending. Err on the side of a shorter playdate with a specific end time.

 Jon and I find it extremely tiresome when playdates end with resistance and whining for more time. At some point we told Laurel (and visiting friends) that—plain and simple—when playdates end badly, it lessens the chance of another get-together (note: we don't threaten that they *never* will happen again because we clearly would never follow up on that). This doesn't mean the resistance and whining never happens, but setting that ground rule helped a lot. When we do meet periodic resistance, we offer a gentle reminder and that tends to dispel the drama.

Communicate with Parents
Playdates are the perfect opportunity to deepen your community. Chat with parents when you drop off your kids or invite them in for a minute when they drop off theirs. Debrief on how the playdate went. Bonding over your kids' friendship can build the foundation for a wonderful reciprocal relationship.

Spontaneous Play in the Neighborhood

Who doesn't fantasize about sending their kids out to play? Lots of people, actually. Modern parenting attitudes are different than they were when we grew up; parents are more fearful about safety, whether because of a need for control, because they live in a busy, urban neighborhood, or because of fear-inducing stories in the media. Sure, sometimes it's not practical or safe to let your kids run around unsupervised outdoors. But if you focus on arming your child with awareness (e.g., what to keep an eye out for, what to do in case of emergency) and work on building neighborhood friendships, your child will have everything she needs to run down the street and ask a friend to play. At some point, your kids will need to navigate the world without you, and independent play is the place to start. Here are some ways to inspire confidence and spontaneous play in the neighborhood.

Invest in Outdoor Equipment

We're not talking major backyard play structure. A back-and-forth sprinkler, a cheap badminton set, a bouncy play ball, or some sidewalk chalk are all you need to get kids playing together. In Asha's neighborhood, an inexpensive plastic saucer swing hanging from a tree in the sidewalk strip has entertained generations of kids.

Teach Your Child Group Games

Hide and Seek, Capture the Flag, Kick the Can…these games never lose their appeal. If you don't know how to play these games yourself, find someone who does (hire an older neighborhood kid to "tutor" if you have to) or look up the rules on the Internet.

Teach Outdoor Safety, Then Give Your Kids Space

Sunscreen, street-crossing rules, neighborhood "wandering" boundaries…all good. Especially when kids get a chance to show their competence. Give them room to roam and explore. Let kids ride their bikes around the block as a prelude to riding around the neighborhood. The knowledge and self-confidence they gain will be tremendous.

Take Up an Outdoor Hobby

If your kids are still too young to be outside alone, build up to playtime independence by using that time to pull a few weeds or admire the neighbor's landscape overhaul. Pull a patio chair into your front yard and read the paper while your kid plays. Communicate your confidence in your kids' abilities by letting them find their own fun.

Reinforce Neighborhood Friendships

If your kid is having a hard time making the leap from neighbor to friend, give him a hand by inviting the entire family over for a potluck or a BBQ. When your child sees the grown-ups chatting and getting to know each other, he may get just the nudge he needs. And you may find a nearby backup, another parent with whom you can trade help when you need it.

Have an Open-Door Policy

Encourage your kid to bring friends home without having to plan ahead. Stash extra snacks in the pantry and a few pizzas in the freezer in case kids want to stay for dinner. Make it as easy as possible for your kid to build neighborhood connections.

When Playtime Doesn't Go Well

For every effortless playdate or neighborhood game of kickball, there's one that blows up in everyone's face. Toys or rules get broken, feelings get hurt, and parents shift around awkwardly not wanting to point fingers or make excuses, but unsure as to what to do next.

Like academic skills, social skills must be learned, and that happens at different rates for different kids. Understanding this, preparing for it, and having a few responses ready for when the firecrackers go off will go a long way toward lowering everyone's anxiety and disappointment.

Most importantly, know that *your child's behavior does not reflect your worth as a parent.* Good kids with good parents sometimes lose it (let's be honest, good parents lose it too)—it's part of learning how to handle the challenges that come with being social. Following are a few tips for handling the explosions.

Separate Damage Control from Problem Solving and Resolution

When kids are riled up, asking them to think logically about the situation (let alone apologize) is unlikely to help. Reserve judgment, and suggest everyone take a few deep breaths. Gently encourage kids to go to their respective corners. Sometimes apologies will have to happen another day (in any case, they're only meaningful when a kid understands why they're necessary).

Don't Hesitate to End the Playdate

Give kids a chance to solve the problem. Sometimes, after they calm down, kids can bounce back and get back to playing as if nothing happened. See if that's possible. If not, don't be afraid to say "Sorry, kids, but playtime's over for now. Let's try this again another day."

Keep Communication Open

Be honest and open. Do your best to tell the other kid's parents what happened (you may not know the particulars), and hold your head high. If your child was in the wrong, acknowledge it and share your response. But try not to let shame enter the conversation. Your kid (and theirs) has a good heart and is learning.

Listen to Your Kid

Once the fires have died down, approach your child to problem solve together. Position yourself as a listener more than a solver. Even if your kid seems like the one obviously in the wrong, listen first to see what prompted the reaction. The tricky thing with behavior is that we tend only to see the problem (someone gets hit or yelled at), not the precipitating event (someone was goading or ignoring). Try to separate the behavior from the problem. Once you identify the problem, you can brainstorm alternate behavior choices.

Do a Run-Through for Next Time

Make sure the apologies and resolution happen. Then do a little rehearsing for the next playdate. You and your kids need to recognize that problems tend to repeat themselves, and preparation and practice is key to solving them.

Playtime is a kid's rehearsal for life. By minimalizing your schedule and opening up free time and space for play and friendship, you're giving your child the most important gift in the world: time to be a kid.

8

Education In and Out of School

If the pregnant/newborn phase kicks some parents into an intense pursuit of perfection, the school years propel that pursuit toward an entirely new and dizzying height. The meandering toddler schedule gives way to the more structured routine of school, and with it comes a whole new category of things to worry about and "get right." Choosing the soundest educational philosophy, competing for slots in the best school, populating future college applications with accomplishments beginning in kindergarten, worrying that one's kid isn't "keeping up". For some, it's a madhouse of anxiety with the added wrinkles of public comparison and one's own childhood baggage.

Since when did educating one's kid turn into a breakneck sprint from infant enrichment classes to high school graduation? Are our kids really in danger of failing adulthood if they don't get straight As at a top school? Are the fear and worry really necessary? (Chapter summary: NO.)

In this chapter, we'll put forth our minimalist approach to your child's education. We're not talking "minimal" education—letting the chips fall where they may and hoping for the best—nor are we knocking parental involvement. Our approach widens the definition of education beyond schooling and lengthens the time horizon beyond the college years. A minimalist take on the school years allows for individual differences in interest and temperament, both yours and your kids'. More importantly, it recasts the educational choices you'll make over the years as exciting rather than scary, because there's always wiggle room. There are so many ways to get it right, because your goal isn't to raise a successful student. It's to raise a successful adult.

Embracing Continual Learning

In the case of our first key of Minimalist Parenting—make room for remarkable—we mean making room for a bigger definition of education. Unlike enrollment slots in a prestigious school, learning isn't bound by scarcity. Embrace the abundance of learning and the peace that comes with it. Once you're confident that your child is learning all the time, you're no longer on the hook to find the "right" or "perfect" school or approach.

Besides, "perfect" is rarely the best setup for learning to occur. Challenges, both academic and of the sort that happen under less-than-ideal circumstances, can often create the most fertile environment for learning. (Getting comfortable with challenge is different from ignoring a bad fit between kid and school; we'll talk about this more later in the chapter.)

Life Is a Classroom

Kids' brains are wired to learn from the first moment they arrive. Every new experience, every bit of exposure, every experiment—whether it's a baby trying out different facial expressions to test which get the biggest reactions to a toddler touching a hot stove to a kid digging in the sand on summer vacation—everything is learning…including (especially) the stuff that doesn't look like learning.

As you begin to toss these sorts of experiences into the pot along with formal school day academics and call the whole mess "your kid's education," you start to realize how big the pot really is. It can hold a lot.

Take a moment to recall your most vivid learning experiences, either as a kid or as an adult. Did some of these moments happen outside of school? Did they involve overcoming an obstacle—and stumbling toward an answer? Are you still learning new things right now?

Mirabai's biggest learning memory so far was when she asked to leave organized swim classes at the local pool so she could teach herself to swim (she was seven years old at the time). Even now, she recalls that experience and the confidence she gained (and the power of trusting her own gut) when learning something new.

Leslee of cr8zygrrlceramics.etsy.com, via the Minimalist Parenting blog: I had a brilliant teacher for high school anatomy and physiology—Donna Mae Huberman—who gave pop quizzes called "Four Sixes." She would bring six students to the front of the class, then ask them questions from that week's lesson. If four of the six students gave correct answers, then everyone in the class received points. Yes, I learned my A&P, but I learned something more important: we are each responsible for the success of the group. Every person has something she can contribute that benefits the class, the school, and society as a whole.

Jarasa via the Minimalist Parenting blog: One learning memory that has stayed with me all my life is my mother's mantra: "There is always something you can learn from everyone you meet. What are you going to learn, what behavior are you going to adopt, from this teacher/friend/enemy/acquaintance?" One learning memory that I wish I had learned as a child in a family where academic success was always the top priority, but am only learning now as an adult, is that "People may not remember exactly what you did or what you said, but they will remember how you made them feel."

As you consider your own learning trajectory, note how long and varied it is (and that it's far from over). Just keeping this in mind may help you dial back some of the worry that you must find the needle of a perfect school in the haystack of choices out there.

That said, your kid isn't you and may have a different trajectory to follow. There are basic academic skills every kid needs to learn, and there *is* college and a future career to consider. Of course this is true.

But we would argue that focusing your attention not on the educational system but instead on your family's unique values and priorities will *better* prepare your child for a world full of competition and choices.

If your kid is safe, engaged, and generally happy, he's learning, no matter what the stats or the test scores or the educational experts say. There's plenty of time to learn skills, but only a few years of childhood to develop a foundation of confidence, problem-solving ability, and flexibility that will make learning those skills (and operating in a fast-changing world) that much easier.

Think about it like this: not so long ago, typing was a major skill taught in school. Knowing how to skillfully operate a typewriter was a benefit when looking for a job. Now, typing is part of the "unofficial curriculum" for the toddlers who are playing on their parents' iPads. The skills will come—it's the wherewithal and creativity to use them that kids need to practice. And they can practice building those muscles in all sorts of environments.

Cultivate a Culture of Curiosity

So where does your newly expanded educational vision leave you? Doesn't Minimalist Parenting call for the narrowing of options, not expanding them to include *everything*? Indeed it does. We'll focus on mechanics in the next section. For now, rejoice in the knowledge that just about everything constitutes learning, not just the "educational" stuff!

We love our *Sesame Street* as much as the next parent, but the reason it's such an enduring educational tool is because kids love it. Which means that *Looney Toons* is also educational, in a totally different way for a totally different kid. Embrace it all (if it fits with your values) and enjoy seeing what comes of it with your kids.

 I was a big fan of the animated series *Super Friends* while I was growing up. You know: Superman, Wonder Woman, and the gang? My favorite Super Friend was Aquaman: THE GUY COULD COMMUNICATE WITH FISH. Looking back, Aquaman was the beginning of my fascination with ocean habitat. When I outgrew Aquaman, it was

Jacques Cousteau, then sea-themed books and art projects. I now drag my family on tide pool quests at every beach we visit in part because of time "wasted" watching Saturday morning cartoons.

Follow up on your curiosity, and encourage your kids to exercise theirs. The subject doesn't matter *as long as you're excited and engaged.* Model a hunger for learning and a willingness to get creative and dig a little to find an answer.

- Explore corners of your town you've never seen before.
- Serve novel foods for dinner (even if they don't always get eaten).
- Read the newspaper comics together—some of our best family conversations start there.
- Hang out at the library; check out books that look interesting. Schedule family reading time, even if that means flipping through picture books for fifteen minutes.
- Listen to different types of music.
- Walk, ride your bike, hike. Anywhere.
- Decide which weeds in your backyard are interesting enough to leave alone and let grow.
- Cook a meal with your kid.
- Grocery shop together.
- Give your kids household responsibilities and praise their effort (even if the results are questionable). Then expect a bit more.
- Insert anything that interests you HERE.

The goal is to give your kids a chance to get comfortable working to find an answer, whether it involves words, numbers, the physical world, or ideas. Mental tenacity is the foundation of learning at every age.

This is a good time to mention extracurricular activities: the myriad classes, camps, workshops, teams, and groups available to modern families. Assuming you have the budget and the transportation, many of these classes offer a wonderful way to expose kids to new things…*within reason.* The pull toward "more, more, more" is strong when it comes to after-school activities. Because of that, we devote chapter 10 to the role extracurriculars can play in a minimalist family life.

Encourage Responsibility and Independence

Another piece of the education puzzle is a kid's understanding of his own competence—the fact that he can, indeed, accomplish good, useful, world-changing things (even if his "world" at the moment is his very messy room). By giving your kids household chores at an early age, you show them that their work matters, and that they are part of a larger system (their family) that relies on their participation.

Chores are a crash course in problem solving (if I put the books away first, my room takes less time to clean), delayed gratification (if I finish my chores I get to watch TV), and skill building (I know how to make my own lunch!), all blocks in the foundation of school and life success. If you let your imagination spin out a few years, you can picture a kid who knows how to operate the washing machine, cook dinner, manage his money, and mow the lawn. Not a bad helper to have around the house, and one who's on track for a smoother transition to adulthood.

We talk specifically about chores in chapter 3, but it's worth mentioning their importance here because they translate directly to schoolwork. It may be hard to see it when kids are young, but soon enough they'll have homework to do, and the more accustomed to independent work they are, the more they will assume homework is their responsibility, not yours. Take it from us, when that conversation happens after school is in session, it's a much harder sell.

Consulting Your Family's Educational Compass

Many parenting experiences bring one's own childhood memories smack dab to the forefront, and school's a biggie. As we approach our kids' school years, we bring along a suitcase full of hopes, fears, expectations, and assumptions. Now that you're looking at education with bigger eyes, it's a good time to examine your unspoken assumptions to see if they fit your minimalist vision of family life...and if they make sense for your kid.

Zeroing In on Your School Assumptions

Take a few moments to recall your own school experience and the familial expectations surrounding it. (This is a good time for your notebook and pencil.) Answer these questions:

- Did you enjoy school? Did you enjoy some years more than others? Why? Why not? Be as specific as you can—your answers will tell you a lot about your school-related preconceptions.
- Did you find teacher approval, grades, and other forms of evaluation motivating or intimidating?
- Regarding school friends: Did you have any? One or two close friends? Lots of friends? Were peers a source of pleasure or resentment? Was peer pressure an issue?
- Regarding your parents' reaction to/involvement with school: What were your parents' attitudes about learning and school performance? Did they care about your grades? Your happiness? Were they involved? If not, did you still feel supported? (This is important: parents don't necessarily need to be actively involved to be present and supportive of their kids' educations.)
- Were you labeled a "good kid" or a "troublemaker"? (Labels aren't always accurate, but they can have a big effect on a kid's self-perception.)
- Did you prefer following your curiosity or getting the right answer?
- Was school an important part of your overall place in your community, either neighborhood-based or otherwise?
- Looking back, would you characterize your school years as "the glory days" or "doing time till real life began"?

As you think about your answers, check in with your inner bus driver (the one you met in chapter 1). What's she telling you? To look forward to and be excited about your child's transition to school, or to worry, be suspicious, and protect?

Your answers—and your assumptions based on your experience—are extremely important tools as you map out your priorities for your child's education. You may uncover a surprisingly positive reaction to strict academics and grades. Or you may discover that most of your school learning was social in nature—the memory of the academics recedes in importance. Your assumptions are unique to your upbringing and environment, and can inform you as you begin to make educational choices.

Identifying Your Family's Educational Priorities

Now that you're aware of the educational assumptions you already have, it's time to turn your gaze outward toward your hopes for your child's education. What is an educated person *to you*? If your kid comes out of his school years with one or two things, what do you hope those would be?

Is your priority creative problem solving? A global perspective and a foreign language? A strong work ethic? Exposure to art and music? A grounding in the neighborhood? What about your partner: Are his or her values different than yours?

Honor these values and your understanding of your child as you familiarize yourself with the educational landscape. Trust your child's resilience; most of the time, she will adapt to whatever environment you choose. (Not always…but there's always time for course correction, which we'll talk about later in the chapter.) Educational philosophies are as subject to fad and fashion as anything else, so don't be afraid to stick to your priorities as you explore school options…there are many paths that lead to a thoughtful, curious, well-informed adulthood.

 To my father, "an education" meant earnest, devoted attention to schoolwork with a focus on the fundamentals of reading, writing, math, and history; respect for authority figures; and an eventual college degree. He grew up in India so didn't have much interest in alternative forms of education or creative expression. My mother grew up in Los Angeles, California, in the 1950s, so her school memories were vastly different. Peer pressure colored her experience of those years, so her concerns spanned school performance and the social environment.

Whenever I needed to ask my dad's permission to attend a social engagement, his response was, "A book is your only true friend." Oh, the irony. I was so eager to fit in with my peers (given the racial and socioeconomic differences I felt so palpably) that I found myself steering away from academics and the "book is your only true friend" mantra (I became a B-/C+ student in high school as a result) because I didn't want to fit the brainy Asian stereotype. This—and my career 180—colors the way I view my kids' education. Of course I want them to do well in school (though mostly because I remember how confusing and painful it was to "not get it" in the classroom), but more importantly, I want them to find what excites them, whether it be science or the arts or something else (as of this writing, Laurel wants to be a cake artist when she grows up).

Factoring In Practicalities: Money and Time

Much as we might like to choose a school based solely on the educational environment, it has to fit into our actual lives. Long drives, high tuitions, and faraway friends can add enough stress to the family system to cancel out whatever benefit the school offers.

As you're looking at your child's school options, consider the independence, exercise, and neighborhood grounding that comes with walking or biking to school. The close-to-home connections and friendships at the local public school are so valuable when your child gets old enough to assume responsibility for his own social life (think: running over to a friend's house to play). Assuming the local school is safe and of reasonably good quality, you can be assured it's filled with a variety of good and bad teachers, programs, and opportunities…as is *every* school.

Choosing a School

You've identified your family's priorities, values, and practical capabilities. Hopefully this has allowed you to narrow down your list of potential schools. If you've reduced your choices to a single school, congratulations! You can skip this section and go make yourself a cup of coffee! But if not, the $64,000 question remains: Which school do you choose?

Good news: there's likely no wrong answer. Each school (including the ones that cost $64,000 per year) has its strengths and weaknesses, its rock star teachers and its duds. You've already done the work of figuring out what's important to and possible for your family—now all you have to do is choose the school that seems most promising. It's really that simple. As you move through this process, try to make room for some new beliefs.

Don't Feel Obligated to Research Every Option Available

Do some Googling, talk to friends, and go on some school tours. When it comes down to it, the final call is best made via your gut (the preferred signal of your inner bus driver). Sending your child to the school that feels best is more important than choosing based on test scores or community reputation. Think about it: you're trusting the school and its teachers with the care and well being of your child. That relationship must begin with a feeling of trust, or it's bound to be tense right out of the gate.

I felt like a loser when I found out that other moms spent months researching and visiting preschools, interviewing teachers, getting their kids on waiting lists, etc. We visited two or three schools then chose the one that felt right. A stroke of luck got our kid a spot in a small, home-based preschool, but looking back now, I know, had it not worked out, he would have been happy and well cared for at another school.

For me, Laurel's preschool choice was rooted in logistics several years before she became a preschooler. Because I was returning to work, I needed a school that offered infant care, which is definitely harder to find, and I wanted to minimize transitions (ideally, an infant care center that continued on up to preschool). As I considered the pros and cons of the prospects, I thought, "These options are all fine. They are clean, safe looking, and it looks like there are plenty of things to play with inside and outside." The school we ended up choosing runs programs from infant to pre-K.

Just before Laurel started preschool, several families transferred out because they wanted a more "rigorous curriculum" (the day care adheres to the learn-through-play philosophy). I remember thinking, "Man, I have no idea what that even means for a three-year-old." I don't know how those kids are doing now—whether their rigorous curriculum has delivered its promises—but I do know Laurel grew and learned so much there and does very well in school now. It has been so great to return to this same day care with Violet.

No School Is Perfect

Every school has its burnt-out teachers, less-than-stellar programs, and classroom troublemakers. Some years will be better than others, both academically and socially. This is *good*. Ups and downs are part of the learning process and help build resilience and tolerance. Ultimately, variability sets kids up for a happier life.

 Sam once had a teacher who was strict to the point of inflexibility. He gave fantastic, well-structured assignments and held his students to high standards, but his delivery was pretty stern. As a result, Sam often bristled at his requests. I know that a gentler approach would have worked better for Sam. But I also know that this teacher is extremely skilled—it showed in the quality of the instruction and the assignments. Sam and I had many conversations about how to work with someone whose personality doesn't "fit" yours. He learned about the concept of "wiggle room"—with some teachers you've got a little, and with others, you don't. Rael and I listened to his frustrations and sympathized with the difficulties of operating within tight boundaries, but we never tolerated disrespect toward the teacher. While I believe that his motivation may have suffered as a result of the tension with this teacher, Sam learned more about his capabilities than he had in any year previous.

The Importance of the Family Support System

We've talked about how everyday learning plays a huge role in kids' development. And so it follows that the environment and support that parents provide their kids (not to mention whatever the kids are going through in their lives socially, emotionally, and academically) can be just as influential as the kids' formal curriculum and instruction (probably more so).

 Given Jon's and my experience, I now believe that the way parents/mentors help shape a child's journey and the child's own readiness/motivation are better predictors of school "success" than school ranking is. I went to a first-rate public high school but I was an unmotivated student. I only got As in music; otherwise, my grades were totally average. It wasn't until I got to college that my academic spark was lit—I was inspired by my professors and the material, and motivated by the fact that I had to put myself through school starting sophomore year. I went on to earn a master's and a PhD, and to finish a postdoctoral fellowship at a trio of Boston's finest academic/medical institutions.

In (initial) contrast, Jon attended a less prestigious high school where he graduated at the top of his class. He went to a top Boston-area college and proceeded to earn two master's degrees. I often joke that our starting points were so different yet we ended up at the same place.

These experiences were critical in framing our approach to Laurel's schooling and to choosing where we lived. Boston is an academic hotbed. People will sacrifice a lot financially in order to live in towns with the best school rankings. But given that Laurel did not appear to have any special learning need, Jon and I felt confident that wherever Laurel went to school—so long as it was clean and safe—would be fine.

Just before Laurel started kindergarten, our lease was up and we were ready to put down roots. We ended up settling in a community ten minutes outside of Boston, where the schools are not ranked as highly as the higher-income surrounding towns. When we told people where we were moving, several asked if we were worried about the schools. But housing was less expensive and we loved the diversity of the community. It has worked out wonderfully. The parent community is amazing, and the neighborhood is incredibly friendly. Laurel is learning and thriving. Her school has more than enough to offer.

The take-the-good-with-the-bad approach to school helps everyone. Your kid comes to learn that she's strong enough to handle a variety of situations, including those that are less than ideal. Your child's teacher will have a partner in you, rather than an adversary. And you can relax, knowing that the natural fluctuations in your child's school experience are building toward her Education with a capital E.

Assessing School "Fit"

Hopefully, your child's school years will go smoothly and the inevitable bumps will be infrequent and relatively small. But what exactly does "going smoothly" mean? Sometimes it's hard to tell because the worlds of home and school can be so separate. Surely, we want more from our kids' school years than for them simply to go by without incident—we want our children to *thrive*. How do you know what "thriving" looks like when your child's week-to-week and year-to-year experience of school varies so widely?

The answer lies in knowing which problems are symptoms of temporary discomfort and which signal a deeper, more persistent problem that requires action. It's a maddeningly moving target, and it requires paying close attention to both your child and your gut.

Evaluating Academic Progress

We all know that kids learn and develop at different speeds. One kid weighs forty pounds on his fifth birthday, while another hits that mark at age seven. One kid begins to read in preschool, while another takes until second grade to hit her stride. The same is true with social skills, maturity, and the ability to sit still, follow directions, and hold a reciprocal conversation... these skills develop at different times for different kids.

But somehow, in school, it's almost impossible to resist comparing your kids to others the same age and then worrying when you see differences, *especially* because comparison and assessment is part of what school's all about. Kids are supposed to hit certain academic "benchmarks" at certain times, and variations in social skills, when far enough from the norm, can prove complicated in the classroom setting (and set you up for more one-on-one time with the principal than you might want).

Think About the Long Term

Put school's academic and social benchmarks into a longer-term perspective. Just because your kid isn't reading at the end of kindergarten or sitting quietly during story time doesn't necessarily mean that there's a problem or a bad fit with a teacher or a school. It may be a simple matter of letting your child's natural development take its course.

Talk to—and Trust—the Teacher

Here's when maintaining open, friendly, trusting communication with your child's teacher really pays off. Not only can you check in with the teacher when problems arise, you can collaborate on a solution. Teachers have the great benefit of watching many kids go through the system, and can provide valuable perspective not only on your child's development, but on differences in behavior between school and home. It's wonderful to know another caring, knowledgeable adult's eyes are on your kid's well being.

 Mira is a conscientious student, and she loves her teachers. When she misses an assignment, it's not due to apathy—it's because her still-developing organizational skills aren't consistent. I take a fairly hands-off approach to my kids' homework—I offer support and structure to get it done, but I leave the work to them. So when I read on Mira's progress report that she didn't turn in an ongoing assignment, I let the teacher know that I was aware of it, and that I'd remind Mira once, but would leave it to her after that. I showed Mira how to use a calendar to remind herself about upcoming deadlines. I gave her a stack of Post-it notes to use as visual cues. We'll see if the assignment gets done. Either way, the teacher supports my prioritizing Mira's independence, and Mira will learn something useful from the experience no matter how it turns out.

Ultimately, Go with Your Gut

Comparing your child with his peers *can* help you identify potential problems if you're already feeling that something's off. It's crucial to keep tabs on your gut here, because you're the one who knows your kid best. You have to walk the fine line between supporting your child, modeling respect for the school system, and advocating for your child if necessary.

Teachers, like everyone, have their biases, and so tend to see "problems" through their own experiential lenses and will respond (and report) accordingly. For example, where one teacher sees a "behavior issue," another teacher will see an anxious child in need of support. Teachers are also constrained by their time, and must attend to the needs of every child in class. Because of these other demands, through no fault of their own, they may miss subtle signals of trouble brewing.

If the teacher insists things are normal but you can't shake the feeling that something's off with your child, don't ignore it—even if you feel intimidated or you worry that you're hovering. We can't stress this enough. Kids are often embarrassed to ask for help. They may not even know how to identify their problem. Think of your intuition as your child's benevolent watchdog, keeping an eye on the situation and assisting when it senses a disturbance.

Involve Your Child

Most of the time, when given the tools and a little direction, kids and teachers can partner to solve problems themselves. Help your child practice advocating for himself—to ask respectful questions, to make reasonable suggestions, to seek out the teacher's help before and after school, and to meet with the school counselor.

If Necessary, Bring in Extra Help

Sometimes your child will need a little more help, either from you or from a school specialist, doctor, tutor, or therapist. Don't be afraid to bring in the help she (and you) needs.

If School's Not Working

What if, despite everyone's best effort, school's just not working? How do you know if the problem is the school, the teacher, your kid, or you? How do you know if it's better to bet on an additional year of maturity and development, next year's teacher, or a new educational setting?

Now's the time to depend on your inner bus driver to lead, because there's no fact-based way to ascertain the "right" answer. The path forward depends on your intuitive understanding of the situation *and* the state of your child. What's right for most kids may not be right for yours, and embracing that takes bravery and confidence. Few among us can resist the desire to fit in, especially when we're used to following the advice of friends and authority figures, and when the alternatives are unfamiliar.

 Sam's early school years were full of struggle. Teachers, friends, and medical professionals all told us that the situation would right itself with structure, maturity, and time. But over the years we watched him sink further into depression and hopelessness. We finally accepted that the usual methods that work for most kids weren't working for him, and we were running out of time. We had to trust ourselves—and Sam—when we made the decision to homeschool him. It was frightening to go against the advice of the authority figures in our lives (including some family members), especially because we had never considered homeschooling an option. But that's where our inner bus driver was pointing. After eighteen months of home-based education, Sam was happier, healthier, stronger, and more confident than ever, so much so that he decided to return to public school and has been thriving there ever since.

Know that, if a particular school isn't working for your child, there are many options for her education and that no choice has to last forever. Course correction beats perfection every time. What's not right now might be right later, and you can make a change should that ever become the case.

Education is so much bigger than school. In the end, the goal is a happy, well-grounded adulthood, and there are many "right" paths and adventures on the way there.

THE ART OF LETTING GO

Early parenting requires such intense caretaking and attention that it's no surprise that it can be challenging for parents to learn to let go of control. But oh how kids thrive when you do. We asked the insightful Ellen Seidman of LoveThatMax.com to share her wisdom on the topic:

Let go of over-therapying your child

My son, Max, has cerebral palsy and cognitive impairment, due to a stroke at birth. He gets a lot of therapy. So for his downtime, I don't load it up with classes, reading time, or intellectually-stimulating anything. As much as I'm tempted to, I let go—and let my son explore what he'd like. Going through a car wash, twice? Sure! Sitting near an airport to watch planes take off? You betcha. Playing an endless game of hide-and-go-seek? Bring it! I step back and let Max tell me what he wants to do and explore. It's ALL good for his brain. It's stimulating, in one way or another. (Well, we do draw the line at letting him watch *Cars 2* five times in a row, which he would if he could.) Max has a lot he can't control in his life, from the stiffness in his arms to his challenges with speech; letting Max control as much of his free time as possible empowers him.

Let go of helping too much

For many years, my husband and I had to spoon-feed Max. He had trouble grasping utensils and getting the food to his mouth. One day, when Max was six, I went to his school to fill out some forms. I stopped by his class to say hi. It was lunchtime, and there sat Max at his desk, peacefully feeding himself. "He feeds himself?!" I asked his teacher, astounded. "Yes, of course!" she said. Hel-lo, codependency! Max was so used to us feeding him that he didn't bother to try at home. When we finally started insisting he do so he resisted, but eventually he came around. It's tempting to step in when Max's physical challenges prevent him from doing things; I so desperately want to help. But in order for him to succeed, I have to help him *less*.

Let go of a timeline

At age nine, Max learned to write his name. The first day he came home from school with "Max" written on a piece of paper, and a note from his occupational therapist that he'd written it himself, I cried. Then I framed it and hung it up in his room. Perhaps others wouldn't be as impressed that a nine-year-old did such a thing. I couldn't be more thrilled. Back when Max was a tot, I tortured myself by reading books and newsletters about child development and milestones. Baby Max wasn't hitting most of them, and I would despair. I finally gave away the books and unsubscribed from the newsletters. I accepted that Max was going to do things in his own time. I am grateful that they happen—not *when* they happen. This, I think, is good advice for any parent. Every child is unique. Every child does things when they are ready to, be it picking up a ball or potty training. Comparing your child to other kids does them (and you) no good. Let go.

9

Strategies for Simplifying the School Year

One would think that the kid-free time opened up by school would leave us lounging in our backyard hammocks sipping lemonade. But so many parents we know find themselves even busier once their kids are in school. How does that happen?

Every parent is busy, no matter how you look at it. But it's worth noting that school comes with its own organizational "overhead." There are lunches to be packed (the ingredients for which need to be stocked in the pantry), outfits to be washed, schedules to be minded, events, conferences, and days off to note in your calendar, pickups to be arranged, social puzzles to navigate, and (for older kids) assignments to be tracked.

Sending your kids to school takes work. Good work, but work all the same. In this chapter, we share some of our best tips for minimalizing the school year so you can more easily devote some of your newfound energy elsewhere.

Creating School Routines

In chapter 2, we talked about the magic of household "autopilot." Predictable routines work beautifully to streamline the rhythm of the school day. When your kids get into the habit of following daily and weekly routines, they'll build a skill that will serve them throughout their school years—especially as workloads and expectations increase.

Think of routines as a long-term fix—they take a while to establish and follow, and they require tweaking along the way. But they're worth the (minimal) commitment and will pay off in spades once everyone's settled in.

Routines are also ideal for helping kids transition *back* into school from summer and holiday breaks.

The Night Before

We've found that the best "getting ready for school" routine begins the night before. Think of it as setting up the dominoes before the effortless knockdown in the morning. As your kids get older, hand the elements of the routine over to them.

Lay Out Clothes

Sidestep "what to wear" problems and "we're out of underwear" laundry fails! If you (or better yet, your kids) lay out an outfit the night before, the morning will go more smoothly.

Detangle Hair

Parents of long-haired kids! You know who you are: the ones struggling with snarls and a grumpy child minutes before it's time to head off to school. Comb out long hair (braid it, even) the night before to tame morning tangles.

Get a Head Start on Lunch Packing

Bag up the nonperishables so all you have to do in the morning is pack the cold or hot stuff. See chapter 12 for more school lunch tips.

Line Up Backpacks and Lunch Bags

Get lunch boxes and bags, along with backpacks or satchels, ready for filling in the morning.

Run and Empty the Dishwasher
There's nothing like waking up to a clean kitchen. With the sink and dishwasher empty, everyone can load dirty breakfast dishes and lunch-making supplies so those precious kids-in-school minutes aren't wasted cleaning up.

Set Out the Breakfast Dishes
We sometimes put the bowls, spoons, cereal, vitamins, and other "breakfast-y" stuff on a tray in the kitchen so it's ready to set on the table in the morning.

Sign Permission Slips, Gather Milk Money, Etc.
Less running around = good. Also, fewer things forgotten!

Get After-School Necessities Together
If your kid has an activity after school, you'll thank yourself for getting the sports uniforms and equipment or other supplies and snacks together in a grab-and-go tote. At the very least, keep a list of supplies on your to-do list so you don't have to remember what to bring along each time.

School Mornings

The keys to a mostly successful morning launch are to *have a plan* and to *stay calm*. Getting sucked into the drama and cranky morning moods escalates the bad feelings all around. Try to project cool confidence (pretend if you must)—hopefully, the kids will take your behavior cues.

How the plan actually looks is up to you and your situation. Variables include the presence of other helpful (and awake) adults, the number and ages of your kids, whether or not you're getting ready for work at the same time, distance to school, and general "morning person" temperaments.

Keep in mind that no routine is perfect out of the gate—routines are meant to be tweaked. No matter how your routine shapes up, the more you model "first we do this, and then we do that," the sooner your kids will do it themselves.

Wake Up Earlier Than Your Kids
Try to get up at least ten minutes before the kids do. Not only do you deserve some alone time with your coffee, you'll feel more in control when the action begins.

Encourage Your Kids to Use an Alarm Clock
Get an alarm clock for each of your kids and begin using it, no matter their ages. The sooner kids get used to waking themselves, the easier everyone's mornings will go.

Susan of emeraldcoastfl.com, via the Minimalist Parenting blog: My first grader was really resistant to getting up, regardless of how many hours of sleep he got. On a random trip to Target, he went gaga over a Darth Vader alarm clock, and our problem was solved. Now, he gets up the minute that clock goes off.

Swap Morning Wake Ups
If your kids have different wake-up times, swap which parent gets up first each morning.

Jon and I have always been big fans of swapping morning wake ups. We started when Laurel was a baby by taking turns getting up with her in the wee hours. It was so much easier to have a restful night of sleep if I knew it was my night off and I didn't need to keep one ear out for the baby. We now do the same thing with Laurel and Violet. Violet tends to get up about an hour earlier than Laurel so Jon and I swap which parent gets up with her. It's so nice when the "Vi alarm" goes off and I remember it's my day to snooze a bit longer.

Say Yes to Breakfast
A good breakfast is a must for a productive school day, and it's a nice time to connect before everyone goes their separate ways. Even late sleepers and those with tiny morning appetites need to eat, so try to make breakfast a priority. Toast and eggs, oatmeal, cold cereal and

milk, fruit, nuts, leftovers from dinner…all good. A hit of protein helps keep brains and bodies going through the morning. For those who can't stomach breakfast first thing in the morning, ask the teacher for permission to send a mid-morning snack.

Preview the Day With Your Kids
Get in the habit of previewing the day with your kids to remind them about upcoming events and tasks, and to get them in the habit of planning ahead.

Hillary via the Minimalist Parenting blog: I make lunch while my kids eat breakfast and we talk about the upcoming day (e.g., remember gymnastics is tonight, so do as much homework as you can at the sitter's after school).

Set Time "Signposts"
Try to break the morning routine into its natural "shifts"—for example, breakfast, getting dressed, brushing hair and teeth, heading out the door. The shifts will be unique to your specific routine. Next, attach times to each shift, such as "breakfast is finished at 8 a.m." Kids can better pace themselves when they're aware of their progress through the routine.

When I was away for a couple of days on a business trip I returned to find one of the chalkboard circles in our kitchen covered with a schedule written by Laurel. Apparently, she decided she wanted to help keep track of the morning schedule, particularly on those days when I was away and Jon had to do both drop-offs. It was rather touching to see this morning ticktock documented:

Wake up and dressed by 7:00
Breakfast eaten, lunch made by 7:30
Pack bags, brush teeth, use bathroom by 7:40
Leave to drop off Vi at 7:45
Finish drop off by 8:00
Arrive at school before 8:35

End on a High Note

No matter how the morning goes down, try to end with a positive send-off. You're working on building habits, and there will be good days and bad days. In the grand scheme of things, progress counts more than straight-line success. Besides, no one will remember the tardy passes in a few years.

After School

We totally get kids' urge to throw off the backpacks and revel in the release from school structure. In fact, we encourage it! But a little routine guiding the after-school hours will help your kids take responsibility for their time, and it will also encourage more relaxed evenings together as a family. If you have a sitter bridging the gap between the end of school and the time you get home from work, involve her in the routine to help make sure that the kids do their homework (you can check it when you get home) and take care of any after-school chores.

Empty Backpacks and Lunch Bags

Identify spots in your home for backpacks to hang (perhaps with the coats) and school papers to go.

 We've got a second-hand coat rack in the entryway and a standing file in the kitchen. When the kids come home, they hang their backpacks and empty them, along with their lunchboxes, and bring everything to the kitchen. Empty containers go into the dishwasher, papers go into the file. When it's time to do homework and sign permission slips or read announcements, everyone knows where to start. (Reality check: it has taken the kids *years* to consistently follow this routine, but at least we're making progress.)

Make Snacks Easy to Grab

Kids are often ravenous when they get home. Instead of getting into the habit of serving your kids snacks—unless that's a job you enjoy—keep an array of healthy self-serve snacks around for kids to grab as needed.

Have Clear Homework and Chore Expectations

Decide up front whether homework gets done right away, after a snack, or during the evening. Same with chores. These expectations can get more flexible as your kids demonstrate their ability to manage their time.

Prioritize Free Time, Exercise, and Rest

No matter what, let your kids know that rest, relaxation, and time to play are just as important as anything they are learning in school. We leave the first hour after school open for rest and free time. Building balance into kids' daily routines sets them up for a balanced working life later on.

A word about after-school activities: consider limiting scheduled extracurriculars. Not only do kids need time off the clock to rest, recover, and integrate a full day of learning, they need opportunities for spontaneous playdates and neighborhood pickup games of Capture the Flag. We'll address extracurriculars more in chapter 10, but keep this in mind as you tweak your family's schedule.

Handling Homework

The official Minimalist Parenting line on homework is that *it ultimately belongs to your kids.* When done independently, homework gives kids practice organizing their time and thinking. You're available to consult and guide (and cheerlead when necessary), but the plan is to gradually remove yourself from the process.

Homework is a mixed bag. Some assignments challenge kids to think creatively, while others might seem like busywork. But no matter what your stance is on the state of homework today, it's here to stay. Consider the conversations you can have with your kids about the purpose of homework, how it fits into each child's schedule, and where it stacks up in their priorities. Talk to them about time management, and how *focused* time spent on homework usually means *less* time.

Homework is also a great place to begin the conversation about pride in one's work. Penmanship, neatness, and attention to details such as "name and date in the upper right corner" are all part of the learning process.

Having your ducks in a row where the mechanics are concerned goes a long way toward simplifying the nightly homework ritual.

Have Supplies at the Ready

Homework goes more smoothly when sharp pencils, erasers, blank paper, a ruler, scissors, a calculator, and a timer are within easy reach. You don't need anything fancy—a basket of supplies sitting on the dining room table or in a closet is fine.

Minimize Distractions

Once homework begins, the snacks, cell phones, toys, and other distractions should be put away. Encourage kids to focus on the task at hand. That said—some kids do better with short bursts of work punctuated by five-minute breaks. The timer can really help here. Do whatever works, but be mindful of how distractions affect the process.

Use Organizational Tools

Consider teaching your kid to use simple organizational tools. Get an inexpensive planner or desk calendar and help your child write his assignments down. Apps can work as well, as long as they don't pull your child into the distracting orbit of the smartphone. Break down larger assignments into milestones, note due dates, and even build in little rewards for finishing. Some kids find using "grown-up" tools very motivating.

Decide If/How to Monitor Homework

As you help your child establish a rhythm of doing homework, you'll need to decide how (or if) you want to monitor that the work is getting done. How you approach this will also depend on your child, as some kids are natural self-starters and others will need some nudging. The ultimate goal is to get your kids into the habit of completing their homework independently, and with care.

 Laurel is definitely a get-her-assignments-done kind of kid. When she was in first grade, she would do her homework first thing after school and I would check it over to see if there was anything that she needed help with.

During second grade, we gave her more responsibility. We told her that homework gets harder to do the later it gets (due to fatigue) but that it's up to her to decide when to do it as long as she gets it done before bedtime. We also told her that it's important to ask for help (from us or a teacher) if she is confused; she doesn't need to feel embarrassed if she doesn't know something—that is the point of going to school!

These methods so far have worked really well. Laurel tends to come home, goof off a little, and then do her homework after she has a snack. She's even done homework with friends during playdates. At the beginning of second grade, she always wanted us to check her work, but by the end of the year, she would only ask us to check her work if she was unsure of a concept.

Maintain a Positive Attitude

Stay upbeat, but also watch for signs of struggle beyond the norm. Even if you're not wild about the assignment du jour, try to maintain a positive front. Most importantly, keep your eyes open about whether your child's attitude toward homework is indicative of a deeper struggle.

Jen of jengraybeal.wordpress.com, via the Minimalist Parenting blog: Establishing a homework routine is just like establishing a bedtime routine, and is just as important! They will have thirteen years of homework before starting college—it will be a big part of their life and it's important to help your kids see it as important. Parent attitude is HUGE here. If you are constantly annoyed that your child has homework, he will develop a bad attitude, too. Keep in mind that sometimes when a kid dreads his homework it is because he can't do it and knows it will be painful to get through. Discuss problems with your child's teacher—there could be a misunderstanding of expectations, a need for tutoring, or something else going on.

Set an End Time

Just as adults need to set an end time to their work and household chores (see chapter 2), kids need an end time for homework.

We set an end time to homework—no matter how much gets done, the books close at 8:30 p.m. so we all have time to reconnect before bed and the kids can get a good night's sleep.

Put Homework Away

When homework time is over, put everything away—supplies and the work itself. This single habit will help kids feel more in control of their homework all week.

Handling School-Related Anxiety

Some kids can't wait for the independence and social buzz that comes with school. But for others, the transition to school is fraught with anxiety and even outright fear. It's heart wrenching to push your kids to do something they don't think they can do. Gentle encouragement toward transition is one of the most difficult conundrums of parenting because it rarely feels good, though it's often the right thing to do.

Laurel struggled with separation anxiety that started in infant day care and lasted through the end of kindergarten. It was hard. Really hard. In kindergarten, we endured colossal freak-outs at drop-off for about six weeks, both at the beginning and end of the school year. It felt as if we would never make it out of the woods, but we just hung in there and stayed focused on Laurel's competence, listened to her with empathy, and stood firm in our support of her teachers and classroom. It was a magical moment when she bounced off to first grade with a wave and a smile.

Following are some strategies to try if your child is reluctant to embrace school independence:

At Drop-Off

You're eager to get the kids off to school and start your morning. But if your child is struggling with anxiety, even five or ten minutes of "transitional assistance" can make all the difference. Plan for extra time during drop off (and schedule your morning meetings to begin 15-30 minutes later than usual) to reduce your own anxiety about getting to work on time.

Remain Calm

Rule number one. When you can manage to stay calm, patient, and supportive, you're removing fuel from the fire of the situation. It's so hard not to show your worry or frustration, especially if you're dealing with daily "I don't wanna!" tantrums, but deep breathing—and keeping in mind how big a transition this is for your child—helps put things in perspective. If you lose your temper—and you will (we all do)—just get down to your child's eye level, apologize, give a hug, and start again.

Listen

Sometimes kids just need to air their feelings, know they're being heard, and understand that what they're feeling is normal. Really, we all feel better when we can have our feelings and effort acknowledged, right?

 Jason via BostonMamas.com: We help our five-year-old find words to express her frustration and feelings. We listen but don't try to solve her problems. I find that helping my daughter become more adept at these kinds of "thinking about feeling" skills helps her so much more than giving her specific advice about a given situation.

 Joan via BostonMamas.com: Tell a story about a time when you started something new (job, project, etc.) and you were scared at first, but you came to love it. It's comforting for kids to know they aren't the only (or the first) person to feel as they do.

Affirm Trust

Some kids experience separation anxiety when they don't yet trust their new set of caretakers. Convey *your* faith in your child's teachers, and reassure her that you would never put her in a situation where you didn't trust the people caring for her.

 Given how much we struggled with Laurel's transition during kindergarten and the disastrous camp attempts the following summer, we laid off camps completely the summer after first grade (instead opting for a babysitter). Given my work commitments, the summer following second grade, I definitely needed to book Laurel in some camps and I wondered how things were going to pan out, particularly given that Laurel's first week of camp was at a program where she didn't know anyone else attending—she had simply opted in based on the content (that, by the way, was a *huge* step for her).

As I took Laurel to her first day, she seemed very calm but I felt I wanted to be explicit about the trust factor...it was a mantra we repeated *a lot* during her challenging transition periods in preschool and kindergarten. I said, "Laurel, the people who run this program have been doing it for a very long time and I have heard really good things. So if you have a question or feel a little nervous or whatever, it's okay to talk to the grown-ups. They are safe. But, if you feel uncomfortable with anything at all, please talk to Daddy and me right away, okay?" Laurel chuckled a little in the back seat and said, "Of course, Mom, I know you wouldn't send me somewhere unsafe. Don't worry!"

As it turned out, on the first day we received the full report from Laurel; she really liked her camp counselor but she thought the drama teacher was "weird." I probed for a more specific definition of "weird"—Jon and I feel it's crucial that she feel empowered to speak up (and trust that she'll be heard) when her gut or experience tells her something is off. It turned out that she didn't like the drama teacher's sarcastic demeanor. All of this is to say that it's important to affirm trust in teachers *and* it's important to let your kids know they can and should tell you if something is (or even feels) wrong.

Send a Reminder

Whether it's a concept (such as kisses from a parent as described in the classic "off to school" book *The Kissing Hand*) or a physical object (such as the family picture locket Christine got Laurel for kindergarten), little reminders of home and family can help ease the transition to school.

Partner with the Teacher

Let the teacher know ahead of time that your child is wary at drop-off time. Make a specific plan for a positive but quick handoff.

Keep Drop-Off Predictable

Have a mini drop-off routine in place so that your child knows what to expect. She's probably feeling extremely anxious, so won't be able to process much else…in this situation, autopilot is everyone's friend. On the way to school, a quiet conversation outlining the order of events can help keep her distracted and calm the "what ifs." "First we'll walk in, then we'll hang up your coat, and then I'll give you a big hug and goodbye kiss, and then Mrs. Lovely will hold your hand and walk you into class."

Remind Your Child to Keep Busy

When you're bored or unhappy, time drags, but when you're busy, time flies. Remind your child about this, and suggest that if she starts to feel sad, she should ask the teacher for a different activity—something to keep her busy so the time passes more quickly. (A heads-up to the teacher will help here, too.)

Make Goodbyes Short

At the end of your drop-off routine, warmly but firmly say goodbye and deliver your child to the waiting arms of her teacher. Try to maintain a soothing "It'll be just fine" demeanor (so difficult, we know).

Arrive Early for Pickup

Commit to arriving a few minutes early for school pickup. Your child will gain so much comfort from knowing he can count on seeing your face as soon as he comes out the door.

Trade Roles with Your Partner

If you find yourself locked into a rough drop-off routine with your kid, arrange to swap with your partner for a while. A little distance might be what both you and your child need to start fresh.

After School

Your kid made it to the end of the day! This is a major accomplishment! If you can, try to avoid running errands right after school so you can take time to reconnect and hear about the school day. If someone else is in charge of school pickup, try to keep the after-school routine simple, predictable, and relaxing.

Play High/Low

Boston Mamas contributor Sheri (a teacher) shared this great tip: ask your child to play "high/low" and tell you the best and worst things about the day. This little game will help your child find ways to cope with the hard stuff, but also recognize the positive. Knowing these extremes will also make it easier to give the teacher a heads-up.

Build In Celebrations and Milestones

Whether it's a small treat, a sticker on a chart, or a five-minute living room dance party, celebrate the end of each school day during the first challenging week or two.

Connect with Friends and Family

Sometimes a phone call to a buddy or an understanding grandparent can work wonders. We've both found that our children seem more willing to dig for the positive spin when talking to friends or relatives.

Don't Dwell

The more you, as the parent, dwell on the negatives, the worse things can get. Try to stay positive and move forward.

Kim via BostonMamas.com: I've learned after three kids to not feed into negativity. There is such thing as giving too much of a forum for feelings—believe it or not, sometimes they just want to sound off and don't need you to make it better. Acknowledge their anxiety but don't reinforce it by giving it lots of attention. You might say "Sometimes I feel nervous when I go to XYZ, but then I'm so proud when I make it through." Then change the subject. Feeding into it validates that they *should* hate it or be worried. Act like it's the most normal thing in the world and then get on with everyone's day.

Thank the Teachers

Make a point to express your gratitude to your child's teachers for their patience and kindness. While most teachers are accustomed to separation anxiety, it still raises the tension level for everyone. Letting them know you appreciate their extra effort makes a huge difference.

Other School-Related Social Challenges

Bullying and other peer-to-peer issues at school are beyond the scope of this book (you'll find our recommendations for books about bullying in the resources section). However, many of the strategies we suggest for handling school anxiety apply. Here are a few more ideas:

Stay in Touch with the Teacher

When there are issues with other kids in the class, let the teacher know. It's easy to assume that teachers are aware of everything going on inside the classroom, but realistically it's impossible to track every interaction. Your input will help the teacher keep a finger on the classroom pulse. Also, when you can keep the teacher abreast of classroom difficulties, he or she can identify learning moments for the kids and also might be able to share some advice on how to help your child handle the situation.

One year, Laurel was bullied by a classmate. Since I never crossed paths with the parents at the schoolyard, I raised the issue with the teacher. She thanked me for letting her know and built in a classroom discussion about personal space and respect later that week. I was so glad I talked to her—having the teacher address the situation in a general way with the entire class not only saved Laurel from being put on the spot, but completely diffused the situation between Laurel and the bully.

Try a Different Medium

Kids won't always be able to articulate what's bothering them. Sometimes, they may be too embarrassed to talk about it. Christine and Jon have found that Laurel can often share difficult issues more easily by drawing a picture or writing something down.

Connect with Parents

Problems between classmates can be diffused and addressed more quickly when the parents in the school community are connected. Sometimes it's tough—for example, if you never see certain parents at drop-off and pickup—but in general, just do your best to get to know the families in your community before problems arise. Over time these touch points will help smooth the inevitable conflicts and awkward moments that happen during the school year.

If you find yourself having to meet a parent for the first time due to a problem between your kids, try to remain open, matter-of-fact, and brief. Apologizing in advance, tiptoeing around the problem, or coming on too strong will only make an awkward situation more difficult. Make it clear that you want to work together to find a solution for both kids.

Getting Connected to the School Community

One of the ironies about the school experience is that, while your laser focus is on your kid, the context is actually collective. Friends, parents, teachers, school administrators, neighbors—this is a team project in a big way, which means there's a wonderful opportunity for community. But it also means *more*—more time spent on school-related activities, more people and schedules to track. Isn't *more* the problem we're trying to solve?

Yes. And the way to solve it with respect to school is to recall one of the keys of Minimalist Parenting: we're in this together. Embracing and strengthening your school community is the key not only to less work, but also to more meaning, connection, and fun.

Drop-Off and Pickup

Ah, the school drop-off and pickup. Sometimes this is the only regular interaction you'll have with your child's school. It can be a time to deepen your "feel" for your kid's experience and maybe even grab a few impromptu minutes with other school parents. Perhaps it's a quick drive-by. Or perhaps it's a moot point—you're at work, so someone else drops off and/or picks up your kids. Whatever your situation, it's worth taking a moment to think about this moment of transition to see if there's an opportunity for building community.

Take Notice of the Other Families Along Your Route
They're prime candidates for pickup and drop-off swaps. Don't limit yourself to people you and your child already know—look for an opportunity to introduce yourself and your child, and see where it goes.

Walk Your Kid to the Door
If you drive, park and walk to the school door with your child. Even a couple minutes together smoothes the transition into school, and it gives you a chance to connect with other parents.

Hang Around
Some of the best friendships are made in five-to-ten-minute increments, so stick around for a few minutes after you send your child off. Introduce yourself to the school's office staff. Scan the bulletin boards outside the office. Familiarize yourself with the faces of the school, including the janitorial and the lunch staff.

Arrive Early to Pick Your Child Up

Same idea—you're opening the door to serendipity. Your next good friend may be standing right next to you.

Get Familiar with Your Child's Classmates

Get to know the kids your child regularly greets. Learn their names and begin to notice how your child's classmates tend to "flock" and hang out together so you have some context for your child's school stories.

Offer to Drop Off or Pick Up Nearby Neighbors

Don't be afraid to call the parents of your kids' friends, or to reach out to families who live nearby. You don't have to commit to a regular setup—Asha has made some good friends (and helped her kids do the same) by offering to be "on call" as a school dropper-offer or picker-upper for families along the route to school. It doesn't matter that the kids don't know each other well or hang out together at school—it's an easy way to help out another parent and to pull the strings of the "village" a little tighter.

Volunteering at School

There's no quicker way to get a feel for the school, the teacher, and the peer culture than to spend time on campus during school hours. Volunteering will also jump-start your face time with other local families. However, it's *not* a foregone conclusion that "good" parents volunteer at their kids' schools. And sometimes it's simply not feasible given work schedules. Check in with your inner bus driver on this one. Ask yourself:

- Will your child enjoy having you at school or does he prefer keeping his "turf" separate?
- Will your presence bring out the happy or the clingy in your kid?
- Do you *want* to volunteer? It's okay to say no, or to say "yes, but only on field trips" (or whatever). There are many ways to help and get involved with school that don't involve volunteering during the school day.

If you've decided that volunteering is for you, check with the office (or your child's teacher or classroom coordinator) about the school policy and how to get started. You might choose a weekly time slot in your child's classroom, or you might work on specific tasks. Perhaps you're the committee type—if so, look into the school's PTA. If you've got event-planning skills, consider working on a school fundraiser or event, or plan a classroom party.

Liz via the Minimalist Parenting blog: Being a full-time working parent, I lose out on the after-school pickup conversations and connections that happen while the kids run out the school door, throw bags at the moms, and then sprint to the playground. To connect with parents within the school community I volunteer a couple hours a few weekends or some late-afternoon work breaks for "special events" in our school—setting up for a Halloween bash, painting murals, cleaning up. The efforts are appreciated by the organizers and I get to meet parents and teachers I may not meet in my class-specific interactions. Additionally, when my daughter entered kindergarten, I befriended a group of moms and we started getting together every month or so for a "Mom's Night Out." It's a great time for us to all get away for a few hours, talk about our lives, and what's going on in school and in town.

When Laurel started elementary school I carried a lot of guilt. My parents were always too busy to participate in school events and I wanted nothing else but for my mom to accompany the class on a field trip or help out in the classroom. And Laurel is exactly the same way; if I could come in every day and perch on the corner of her desk she'd be thrilled.

My guilt stemmed from the fact that I work full time (actually, more than full time) yet because I work out of a home office, I felt l ike I "should" be flexible and volunteer. At some point I told myself that it was time to let that go and simply focus on contributing where I *wanted* to contribute, whether that was bake sales (because I love baking) or helping to sew a class banner (since I'm really good at sewing rectangular things). It was liberating to realize the judgment was completely in my own head. It also helped to realize that when it comes to parent involvement, truly, every small act is appreciated.

 Susan of emeraldcoastfl.com, via the Minimalist Parenting blog: We're bus people, and have been since kindergarten, so I missed that before-school pickup and drop-off chat with other parents. I generally let my son take the lead. Once he identified some friends, I would reach out directly to parents to set up playdates. I also tried to pop in for lunch once a month or so, and tried to attend most special events. Our teacher was really good about scheduling things first thing in the morning so work-outside-the-home parents could stop in before work.

Whatever you choose, be sure it's an activity you enjoy. If volunteering starts to feel like a chore, your child will sense your ambivalence and much of the value will be lost. If that happens, it's best to follow through on your commitment, and then find a different way to support the school.

The logistics and emotional underpinnings of your child's school year are a huge part of your parenting experience. By applying a little organization, and balancing the support you provide with the independence you're encouraging, you can participate in your child's education while still reserving time and mental space for your other priorities.

10

Beyond the Schoolyard: Enrichment and Extracurriculars

Comedy camp! Trapeze lessons! Indoor soccer leagues! These are abundant times. If you have the time and money, there are countless enrichment programs and extracurricular activities for your kids to try. Ironically, however, the vast array of extras can translate into day-to-day scarcity...of time and energy and relaxation. Not only for your child, but also for you, the designated chauffeur between activities who also wonders how to get dinner made, homework supervised, and a clean outfit ironed for work tomorrow.

Don't get us wrong: classes, camps, sports teams, and interest groups are a wonderful way to expose kids to new experiences and friends. But there comes a point of diminishing returns: when each commitment added to the schedule generates more stress than learning—or even fun.

By now, it's obvious that we're fans of open space—as it applies to your house, your schedule, and your life. Minimalizing extracurricular activities takes into account your family's interests, energy level, and budget while making plenty of room for creativity and free play. In other words, we encourage you to just say *no* to overscheduling.

Putting After-School Activities into Perspective

We all want our kids to have fun, get active, and be exposed to different ideas and experiences. But it's worth taking a critical look at what actually contributes to the development of a well-rounded person. When we think of an ideal "well-rounded" adult, this person has an array of interests *and* a balanced life. She's involved, but not on the constant go-go-go. She makes time for activities and for quiet. Sometimes she's "doing" and other times "being." She sees the value of both social time and private time (with family and alone).

Contrast this with the life of many modern schoolkids: rising early for school (some even earlier still so they can finish homework or go to sports or music practice), busy most weekday afternoons and evenings with sports and activities, rarely home for dinner, cramming homework into snatches of time that are left…often sacrificing sleep to do so. Weekends are just as packed. Playdates are nearly impossible to schedule, and pickup basketball in the neighborhood? Forget it. Some kids even forget how to fill their own time, becoming anxious and antsy without a programmed activity to occupy them.

The Motivating Power of Boredom

You know how "necessity is the mother of invention?" Well, boredom is the mother of mud pies and killer neighborhood games of Capture the Flag. When kids are too busy to be bored, they miss the biggest creative motivator around.

We're not exactly suggesting that you build boredom into the schedule…more that you don't fear it. Let boredom become your ally. It may take time for your kids to come around, and you'll need to steel yourself against protests, but the skill of self-entertainment is a long-term win.

 My favorite answer to complaints of boredom: "Congratulations! That's the signal that you're about to get really creative!" It merits an eye roll from the kids, but it's sinking in.

Will Your Kids "Miss Out?"

There are fantastic benefits to being involved with a sports team or music lessons. But only when those activities are part of a balanced life that includes open time for play, chores, reflection, family togetherness, and rest. If you think about it, a schedule crammed with activities runs the risk of a different kind of "missing out"—missing the chance to identify one's interests, community, and self.

Having too many scheduled activities cuts into your child's ability to pursue and build friendships. An activity is a great way to *meet* new friends, but *deepening friendships* requires time and space to get to know each other.

Another casualty of overscheduling: household responsibility. Many parents reduce the stress on their super-busy kids by prioritizing the time left for homework while lowering expectations about chores and family involvement. Yes, something's got to give…but it shouldn't be chores. Chores are at the foundation of learning collective responsibility and represent real skills kids will take into adulthood and real delegation potential for you. Free "extracurricular enrichment" in the comfort of your own home! (We delve into the importance of chores in chapter 5.)

Other gems that tend to fall by the wayside of a too-busy schedule: reading for pleasure; arts and craft projects; quiet brain-building activities such as jigsaw puzzles, board games, and solitaire; jaunts to the park; spontaneous weekend adventures; and imaginative and integrative thinking time that can't be quantified.

Finally, it's worth tossing in a little parent-of-tween perspective. *Childhood goes by quickly.* Soon enough you'll find yourself wondering where the time went, and wishing you had a bit more. During the clamor of everyday life, it's all too easy to overlook just how precious those after-school hours are. If your kid still wants to hang out with you, grab those hours and make the most of them, even if that includes watching through the kitchen window as your kid mows the lawn.

Before You Sign Up, Ask Yourself Why

These days, the unspoken assumption is that you'll sign your kids up for after-school activities. Many parents question the safety of letting kids play outside unsupervised. People feel pressure to "prepare" kids for competition, whether on the playing field or for future college admission. Many parents rely on after-school activities to serve as the bridge between the end of school and the time they get home from work. Some simply resign themselves to substituting organized activities for after-school play because there are no playmates left who have any free time.

But before you sign your kid up, ask yourself why you're doing it. Really, why? Is it because your kid has a burning desire to play soccer or guitar? If yes, then fantastic! Step right up! But if not, perhaps there's another reason you feel compelled to fill the schedule. We've touched on some of these motivators in previous chapters, but they warrant revisiting here:

- Are you trying to make up for opportunities you missed as a child?
- Do you equate signing your kids up for lessons with being a better, more caring parent?
- Are you suffering from FOMO—fear of missing out? Are you afraid your kid will be excluded from the "in" group of kids...or that you'll be left out of the "in" group of parents?
- Does unstructured time (with potentially bored children) make you nervous?

No need to feel guilty or sheepish here—there's real pressure to conform, and we're all vulnerable to it. We *all* want to give our children wonderful experiences. But when you get honest with yourself about the motivations behind your actions, you can make better-informed choices for your entire family.

Assessing Your Child's Interest and Readiness

When it comes to "fun" and "interesting," every kid is different. Obvious? Maybe, but you'd be surprised how easy it is to lapse into "every kid should learn a musical instrument" generalizations. Your kid's best friend may love improv classes, but they may be your child's worst nightmare.

The same goes for scheduling. You may have a child who thrives with a different after-school activity every day. Or you may have a kid who wants little to do with formal programming. Or your kid might just be the sort who resists anything new.

Listen to your kid even if he's not sure of himself. Give his interests more priority than yours. When you try to force your own preferences on a resistant kid, it won't go well for anyone. On the flip side: open your mind. You might discover that your child wants to pursue something you'd never considered.

My kids both prefer free time after school, so we've never been big on the extracurriculars. But one day, while talking about interests with Mira, she surprised me: "I've always wanted to play the fiddle!" (Always? She was eight at the time.) Our family loves music, and her dad had been dabbling with the mandolin, but (to me, at least) her interest in the fiddle came out of left field. She had never mentioned it before. I made appreciative noises but didn't rush to sign her up for lessons, thinking that her "interest" was more of a passing fancy. Weeks went by, and she would quietly, but consistently, ask if I had looked into violin rentals or teachers. When two months passed and she was still asking about it, we decided to take the plunge. Fortunately there was room in the budget and the schedule, because she wasn't doing anything else. We found a local teacher, and she has been practicing and playing ever since. The motivation and excitement shines because the idea was hers.

Sometimes, getting at your kids' preferences is easier said than done. They might not be able to verbalize the rationale behind their choices, which makes it hard to know how to proceed. On one hand, you don't want to force a kid to do something he dislikes, but on the other, you want to encourage him to expand his comfort zone. It's an art more than it's a science. Sometimes being "ready" takes longer than you expect.

Extracurriculars for Laurel are one area where I have had to work hard on doing an explicit "why" check. As a child I wanted to do everything when it came to extracurriculars and was allowed nothing (save music lessons—a "productive" extracurricular—later on down the road) because we had a large family and a tight budget. So when Laurel started elementary school and program options started cropping up, I wanted to offer her the world. Or at least have her try something. *Anything.*

But Laurel was extremely resistant to activities of any kind. For a very long time. Our initial forays into swimming and ice-skating were agreed to reluctantly and resulted in tears and freak-outs on the way to and during lessons. It's awful to watch your child sob (quietly... or sometimes really loudly) while standing amid a huddle of kids who are having a great time.

So I finally gave up. I decided that I would simply put the options out there and let Laurel lead.

For a long time, when I asked Laurel about yet another incoming extracurricular flyer from school, the answer was *no*. But when she finally said yes to soccer, she did so with a glimmer of excitement and enthusiasm that carried from that day to the sporting goods store and finally out onto the field for practices and games.

As I watched Laurel run around—a gleefully squealing part of the moving soccer amoeba—it occurred to me that some kids just take longer to settle into their bodies. All of a sudden Laurel was demonstrating a level of comfort and agility I hadn't seen before. It was worth the wait.

Handling Super-Motivated Kids and Intense Commitments

While some kids take a while to feel around and decide what they are ready to pursue, others are ready to leap out of the gate with tremendous self-motivation and talent. How do you maintain a Minimalist Parenting approach when you're faced with the possibility that your kid might be the next violin prodigy or gymnastics star? How do you progress toward a minimalized life when you know that the deeper your child gets into a given activity, the greater the time and expense drain will be?

Letting Kids Find Their Inner Bus Drivers

One of the wonderful things about letting kids find their way—instead of pressing activities you would like to see them pursue—is that they might discover passions and talents you would never have identified.

 My tendency with Laurel has simply been to throw options against the wall and see what sticks. And while she didn't gravitate to sports until later, it became clear early on that Laurel showed deep focus and interest in doing things with her hands—she can sit for hours working on art projects or elaborately frosting and decorating cakes.

I plan to use the same approach with Violet. Even though she is only a toddler, she's already showing signs that she is extremely physical and fearless in nature (read: she throws her body around with a joyful abandon that we didn't see in Laurel). I'll be curious to see if that holds as she grows or whether we'll find that something completely different sticks to the wall.

If your child shows remarkable talent and self-motivation, we say let her go for it—be as supportive as you can within the parameters of *what works for you and the rest of your family.* It can be amazing for a child's growth when her parents support her commitment to a pursuit that requires a lot of time and effort. We do recommend, however, that you keep watch over the temptation to take over steering your child's bus.

Recognizing When You're Pushing Too Hard

When you see your child start to show a talent or interest in something, it's natural to want to nurture that interest. But at some point, you might find yourself pushing your child to do more and more, to be the best, to earn the title of "gifted."

Depending on your child's personality, he may just go along for the ride and won't make a peep. Or he may continue along but turn resentful and brooding. Or he may finally say, "ENOUGH. I quit."

It's hard to pull back from what looks like glimmering opportunity for your child. Pursuing mastery of any sort will involve both fun and challenge, and sometimes it's wise to push your kids through the hard moments. But you must remember to listen to not only what *your* inner bus driver is telling you, but to what your child's inner bus driver is broadcasting. If you find that you're the one driving the bus toward the cliff, it's time to put on the brakes.

Recognizing When To Push a Little Harder

You've driven your child to and invested money in countless lessons and practices. She seems really good at it (whatever *it* is). Like, *really* good at it. But now, all of a sudden, she wants to quit. It's tricky to figure out when to encourage your child to stick with something and work through the hard stuff...and when to let it go.

No one wants the label of "quitter," but it's important to recognize that sometimes, after trying something for a while, kids might simply decide they don't want to do it anymore. We've all had hobbies or projects we've tried but ultimately decided to let go, and kids need the space to make those choices as well. On the other hand, sometimes kids hit obstacles they see as deal breakers, but you know that, once addressed, could breathe new life into the child's interest. Each situation has its nuances, but in general, we recommend reflecting on why you want your child to stick with the activity in question, and also digging deep with your kid about why she wants to quit.

 I started playing violin in the third grade through my school's public program. My parents were able to make the financial commitment to renting a violin but could not afford private lessons. My mom was the motivating factor: she loved the instrument and owned a full-size violin that she bought during nursing school but never had the chance to learn (given that not long after nursing school she married my dad and started to have a bajillion babies). I was so happy to finally participate in an extracurricular activity that I eagerly said yes to learning violin.

I felt so proud when I carried my violin case to school every week and I showed some natural musical ability. However, I was also frustrated that I couldn't improve more quickly. I now know that this is part of my personality—when I start something, I want to go from beginner to expert, well, at warp speed. I wasn't progressing quickly enough with only a weekly in-school group class.

Toward the end of fifth grade I told my mom I wanted to quit. We had a colossal argument about it. I mean, *colossal.* For me, there were two issues: the not-accelerating-fast-enough issue and the fact that all of my friends were planning on singing in the chorus in sixth grade. I desperately wanted to be part of the herd.

Though it wasn't the most nuanced or relaxed conversation, the bottom line is that my mom refused to let me quit. She told me it was ridiculous to change music paths just because of what my friends were doing *but* that she would find a way to help me get lessons to see if that would solve the acceleration problem. I was still angry that she forced me to continue violin, but I relented.

I have no idea how she did it, but when I started sixth grade, my mom found the money for me to start taking weekly private lessons. I was well behind on the competitive music track some of my peers were on but I accelerated fast. I started auditioning for and participating in competitive orchestras. *I loved it.* I played solos in the school orchestra and during college played solo recitals without a modicum of jitters. I continued on to play in a semiprofessional orchestra during graduate school.

I no longer play violin, but I've said many times that I'm so glad my mom didn't let me quit. She saw talent that I didn't know I had and she helped me work around the issues that were getting in the way of realizing my potential.

Setting Activity Limits

If your child wants a full dance card, keep in mind that these activities impact several people: siblings, friends, your partner and you. As keeper of the checkbook, dealer with the details, and driver of the car, you have veto power. One kid's after-school schedule must work for the whole family.

Your child has a lifetime to explore and experience; he doesn't need to explore every option *right this second*. It's okay to "back burner" certain activities in order to protect some downtime, knowing they'll still be available next year. And if they're not, something else will be. In the meantime, your child will learn to be flexible and that his actions and activities affect other people.

Handling the Logistics of After-School Activities

Once you've settled on an after-school activity that works for you and your kid, there are plenty of ways to efficiently work it into your schedule.

Prioritize Nearby Activities That Begin Soon After School Ends

We've had the best success with activities that are in the neighborhood and that begin right after school. (The best ones happen on school grounds right after the bell rings.) The longer the transition between school and activity, especially when it involves time at home, the more likely it is kids will lose energy and poop out.

Disperse Activities Across the Week

If your child likes to have more than one after-school activity per week, try to disperse these activities across the week (e.g., Monday, Wednesday, Friday) to build in open time and also give you a break. Yes, this means that your child may not get her top choice of activities, but that's okay, too (it's yet another chance to learn flexibility).

Sign Up and Swap Driving with a Friend

For many kids, joining an activity with a friend lowers the anxiety, ups the bonding, and increases the fun. For you, the bonus is potential ride sharing! Offer to trade rides with a parent—that way, you'll both get to participate and observe, *and* you'll get a little extra free time in the bargain.

Run Errands Nearby

Many classes and lessons only involve you as an observer. There's no rule that says you have to watch every moment of every class. Run a quick errand nearby, excuse yourself to make a phone call or two, or use the downtime to read or do a crossword puzzle.

Involve a Babysitter

If after-school activities are a child-care bridge to the end of your workday, you may be able to hire a local babysitter just to pick your child up from school and shuttle her to her activity and then home.

Be Okay with a Day Off

There are bound to be days when your kid (or you) is too tired, hungry, cranky, or busy to participate. Decide up front that it's okay to skip a day here and there. While it's important to follow through on a commitment, it's also important to honor one's need for an occasional break (yours or your kid's).

 Natalie via ParentHacks.com: Too frequently, I would sign my daughter up for an activity she enjoyed, but then she would resist going. I couldn't figure out why, but after a bit of discussion it was apparent that she just didn't want to go. If I forced her to participate, she would become upset and cry, yet it made no sense to let her skip for no reason. It's so frustrating to spend money on these activities only to have such resistance when it is time to go!

My solution was to give her one "personal day" per session. She could skip one class per session, no questions asked, but then she had to attend the rest of the classes. It worked wonderfully! She didn't even use her personal day most of the time. I think just giving her some control over the situation made all the difference.

Special Considerations for Summer

Many parents stress out in anticipation of summer scheduling (sometimes starting right after the winter holidays). What if the camps fill up? What if we're stuck doing nothing all summer? What if my kid forgets everything he learned during the school year?

While it's a good idea, particularly if you work full time outside of the home, to schedule summer programs well in advance, try not to worry too much about building the "perfect" summer agenda. As circumstances and schedules shift, trust that there is enough summer programming to fill the gaps, even if that means hiring a sitter or setting up some extra summer playdates. There's nothing more frustrating than killing yourself over planning summer down to the minute only to have something change, leaving you to watch several hundred dollars' worth of deposits go down the drain.

 Laurel attended a full-day, year-round day care (three days a week) preceding elementary school, so when we were faced with the public school calendar, with its shorter hours, week-long school year vacations, and summer vacation months, I was admittedly a little (okay, a lot) freaked out. So, well in advance of the end of kindergarten I booked several weeks of summer camp; I admit that I did this based on my schedule needs and didn't consult her on programming.

As the school year began to wind down, Laurel went through a phase of incredibly difficult transitions during school drop-off and pickup. Her transition difficulties persisted through two weeks of summer camp, which made the drop-offs there enormously stressful as well. What's more, the anxiety around those drop-offs spilled over to the rest of the day (e.g., difficulty at bedtime in anticipation of the next day's drop-off).

Those two weeks of camp felt like the longest two weeks of my life. By the end, I was glad that the other two weeks of the camp had been cancelled (it was originally a four-week camp). We talked to Laurel about what she wanted to do going forward and she said, definitively, "Stay at home."

So, I ended up canceling (and eating the deposit) the other camp weeks we had booked at a different location and instead hired a sitter. Laurel was incredibly happy. The relaxed pace at home gave her the time to recover from the stress of the last couple of months of kindergarten and camp. By the time she headed to first grade, it was as if a magical switch had flipped. On the first day of school I braced myself for a colossal freak-out. It never happened. Laurel looked a little nervous, but no more so than the other kids. She gave me an encouraging wave and a smile and marched off with her class. She was fine. I, on the other hand, had tears in my eyes.

Finally, the summer is a great time to teach your kids about earning money or participating in the community. Help your kids set up a lemonade stand or, for older kids, help them find volunteer opportunities or a summer job. These types of work and community activities are most definitely enriching for kids, even if (perhaps especially if) they're not always easy. (Browse chapter 6 for more advice about teaching kids money management skills.)

When thoughtfully chosen, extracurricular activities can be a fantastic addition to your child's education, as long as you remember they're optional.

11

Meal Planning For Real Life

Food is at the foundation of parenting. We all need to eat, and we all deserve to enjoy it. But the bar on family meals has gotten a lot higher in recent years, with health scares about childhood obesity and nutrition, worries about the developmental importance of family meals, and the ever-present food- and homemaking-perfection imagery in the media. Add to that the time it takes to pull off serving a balanced meal, and it's no wonder that feeding the family ends up feeling like yet another task on a very long to-do list.

Choosing, shopping for, preparing, and enjoying our meals is at the center of family life, so it stands to reason that it should nourish more than our bodies. Mealtime can and ought to be an enjoyable, integrated part of the family system. By streamlining the process, bringing expectations down to earth, and injecting some fun, you'll increase the odds of getting good food on the table and enjoying it with your family.

Feeding Your Family with a Minimalist Mind-Set

We love food. I mean, we *really* love it. But we're not immune to the factors that can turn meal making into a chore. It's no wonder we're feeling a little inadequate: it sometimes seems as if one needs a degree in nutrition to keep up with all the changing standards and a year in chef school to turn out five gourmet meals per week. But such expectations don't reflect reality! You can eat well, enjoy mealtimes with your family, and stick to a reasonable grocery budget without having to jump through every nutritional and culinary hoop. It all starts with you.

How Do You Feel About Food?

Before you start planning next week's meals, take a few minutes to acknowledge your feelings about food and cooking, because they'll guide the planning process. Ask yourself:

- Do you enjoy cooking or would you rather "assemble and heat" or get takeout?
- Do you enjoy eating or are you just as happy to grab whatever's available as long as it's filling and relatively nutritious?
- Do you consider grocery shopping a fun outing or a dreaded chore?
- Are there particular meals you like to prepare more than others? (Perhaps you're a lover of big breakfasts or a whiz with the grill?)
- Do you enjoy planning meals in advance, or do you prefer to let what's in season inspire your cooking?
- How would your partner answer these questions?

There are no wrong answers here. If cooking relaxes you and brings you joy, great. But don't feel guilty if food isn't your cup of tea—there are plenty of ways to feed your family well without devoting yourself to the kitchen. Knowing and accepting your unique baseline is always the place to start.

What's Your Family's Situation?

Let's think practically for a moment. How do the dinnertime hours look for you and your family? Two working parents who pick the kids up from child care at 5:30 p.m. every weekday have very different needs than a family with an at-home parent and three kids under four years of age.

Ask yourself these questions about your family's situation:

- What time do you and your partner get home each day? Do you need meals you can throw together quickly, or is someone home to get dinner started earlier in the day? Does one of you regularly get home after dinnertime?
- How much hands-on help do your kids need during mealtime? Are you working with high chairs and baby food, or are your kids cutting up their own waffles and pouring their own milk?
- What about after-school activities? Are the predinner hours spent shuttling kids to practices and classes? Are the kids even home at dinnertime?
- Does anyone in your family have special dietary needs?

Every family's answers will look different. You may even find that your answers cause you to take a second look at some of your family's choices about work schedules and extracurricular activities. Or not! If you're happy with how your schedule is laid out, there's a way to feed your family that will work with it. Yes, sit-down dinner is lovely and it's something we consider to be an important touch point. But it is *not* a nightly requirement for a well-connected family and well-adjusted kids.

 We've never been big on after-school activities in my family, simply because my husband and kids need lots of unstructured "recovery" time between school, work, and other activities. We're also both fortunate enough to work at home, so long commutes don't affect our mealtimes and we sit down to dinner together most every night. But I know other families who juggle multiple kids, jobs, and sports activities, and dinnertime for them looks like a buffet with a revolving door. It takes planning, but they make it work beautifully—while dinner warms in the oven or slow cooker, kids come and go, sharing a meal with whichever parent is on duty that evening. They have their big family meal every Sunday evening—and it's "breakfast for dinner." They schedule their mealtime family connection for a time that naturally fits into their family's rhythm.

Getting Your Family Fed with a Plan

Now that you have a good sense of your feelings about food and the practicalities of your family's overall situation, you can map out a minimalized plan for getting everyone fed.

Planning Meals: Keep It Simple

When you hit the grocery store without a plan, you can spend an hour shopping only to return home feeling as if you have nothing to eat. Somehow, the granola bars, apples, broccoli, and milk you bought are not magically coming together as a meal!

Meal planning takes a few minutes, but it will save you hours (and stress) during the week. Even so, it's easy to let it fall by the wayside. A good way to start is to plan the week's meals before you hit the grocery store. Even if you prefer to shop and cook seasonally, having even the bare bones of a plan will save you so much time and mental bandwidth. Write your menu ideas on a piece of paper (Asha uses the flip side of her shopping list) or plug them into your calendar.

Start by Looking at Your Schedule

Which nights are busiest for your family? Plan on leftovers, slow-cooker meals, takeout, or super-easy meals (breakfast for dinner!) on those nights.

Keep Meals Simple

No need for complicated entrees, coordinating side dishes, and home-made desserts. Simple food—quick pastas, simply seasoned broiled meats, and stir-fries—is easy to prepare, easy on the pocketbook, and easy to love. Mealtime accompaniments can be as simple as a platter of cut veggies and fruit, a bowl of baby carrots, or a pot of steamed rice. Come up with a few meals based on pantry or frozen items so you can always have the ingredients on hand.

Involve Your Family in Meal Planning

In order to increase the likelihood that people will eat (and enjoy) what is being prepared, and—perhaps more importantly—to spare you the responsibility of meal planning solo, get everyone involved. Survey your family for meal ideas. The nice thing about this approach is that invariably someone thinks of a great dish that the family enjoys that hasn't been in rotation for a while.

Make the Meal Plan Visible to the Whole Family

Write down the suggestions somewhere easily visible. Christine likes to use the adhesive chalkboard circles in her kitchen, but the back of an envelope taped to the fridge or tacked to a corkboard works just as well.

Embrace Repetition

Once you find a meal your family likes, repeat it! Most families look forward to a little predictability. You might even consider the old-fashioned-but-helpful meal-per-day approach (Monday: pasta, Tuesday: chicken…). You can even repeat entire weekly meal plans.

While writing *Minimalist Parenting,* I decided that I needed to vastly reduce the amount of time and creative energy I spent on the weekly meal plan. I came up with a simple menu that repeated each week, including a meal built around a weekly rotisserie chicken. The plan also included neighborhood meal swaps: my neighbors and I shared the job of buying the chickens, salad, and bread and delivered them to each others' houses each Monday. My kids' reaction to certain meals was lukewarm, but we talked about balancing my need to simplify the plan with their need for nightly favorites. In the end, they understood the compromise, even though they weren't particularly thrilled about it.

Don't Forget About Lunch

Whether for yourself or your kids, don't forget to plan some lunch options and make sure you add those items to the grocery list. We minimalize lunchtime (both at-home and packed for school) in the next chapter.

Add Extra Fruits and Veggies to Your List

We all could probably stand to eat more fruits and vegetables. Even if you don't have a specific purpose for them, pick up extra fruits and veggies for snacking and bolstering leftovers. If you're worried they won't get eaten, consider good-quality frozen vegetables.

Plan for Double Portions

Certain meals, such as casseroles, soups, stews, and roasted vegetables, are worth doubling up. The prep isn't much harder, but the result is another meal! Freeze leftovers for future meals or as components for meals later in the week.

Getting Help: Meal-Planning Services

If meal planning fills you with tension, there are some fantastic, reasonably priced services—for example, The Six O'Clock Scramble (thescramble.com) and Relish (relish.com)—that will do the meal planning for you. They generate the plan, the shopping list, and the recipes, and all you have to do is shop and cook. Most services are flexible enough to handle different dietary requirements and preferences.

If you're shaking your head thinking, "There's no way my picky kids would go for that," consider that it might be an ideal way to introduce your family to new foods.

My kids are so much more receptive to meals that get served because they're "on the plan" rather than because of my nutritional or culinary whims. Somehow having a neutral third party (the plan!) calling the shots changes the entire situation.

Streamlining Grocery Shopping

Now that you have your menu plan, it's time to hit the store. Here are some things to keep in mind:

Don't Forget the Grocery List

Once you embrace meal planning, your grocery list will be easier to generate. You can write up a new list each week, replenishing staples and supplies as you go along, or you can use a preprinted list you check off throughout the week. The beauty of posting a preprinted list? The whole family can add items as they notice the need.

I post a list on the fridge and encourage the whole family to add items. I then only buy what's listed. Not only does it keep the grocery budget in check, it prompts my kids to step up and use the list if they really want something. Long-term, this also prepares them to do their own weekly grocery planning once they move out.

If Tech Helps You Streamline, Go for It

Some people prefer handwritten lists; others prefer smartphone apps.

Maddie via the Minimalist Parenting blog: I use GroceryIQ, a free grocery shopping app that occasionally offers coupons, to keep track of my grocery list. I share the account with my boyfriend, who can see the automatically updated list sorted by store. No more calls to ask if we need anything from the store! I also keep a recipe archive in Evernote. (I'm starting to sense a theme here: my grandmother had recipe cards, I have Android apps.) I link directly to the recipes and sort them in categories that I can refer back to when I'm making a grocery list. Having that list and sticking to it keeps our grocery bill down to very reasonable levels (even for New York!).

Shoot for Shopping Once a Week

Meal planning will help you reduce the total time you spend grocery shopping because you'll have an accurate list of everything you need to get you through the week. Consider shopping at an all-in-one grocery store that includes household items as well. Remember—your time is valuable, and it might be worth compromising on the exact food item to save you a shopping trip.

Know Your Stores and Space Out the Trips

If shopping at a single store just won't work for your family food- or budget-wise, split your shopping into multiple trips on different days. That way you can pick up any forgotten items later in the week at the second store.

Consider "Supplemental" Grocery Shopping

Is there a grocery store you can hit during in-between pockets of time? Say, while your kid is at soccer practice? With a menu plan and grocery list in hand, you can accomplish plenty in twenty minutes.

Investigate Healthy Convenience Foods

Supplement your cooking with healthy, ready-made items. Frozen vegetables have gotten a lot better over the years and, unlike the fresh versions, they don't shrivel in your vegetable crisper and you don't have to chop or wash them. Also, frozen fruits and vegetables are picked and frozen at their peak so they taste pretty good! Premade fresh salsa, hummus, and dips can turn a bowl of rice and beans or cut veggies into a meal or side dish. Asha's local natural food grocery puts roasted organic chickens on sale once a week, and they end up costing the same as if she were to buy raw chicken and cook it herself.

Say Yes to Bulk Buying

Convenience foods are great, but are they worth the money? Some bulk items such as dried beans and grains—which initially seem like more work—are actually easy to fit into the weekly plan, especially if you use your freezer. Boiling a pot of beans takes time but very little prep or attention, and the cooked beans can be frozen for later use. Same goes for grains such as brown rice.

A caveat: if your definition of bulk buying includes a 128-ounce jar of mayonnaise from the warehouse store, you're wise to consider the mental "cost" of having to rearrange your refrigerator contents to house it, come up with ways to use it up, and clean and recycle the empty container.

Outsource Grocery Shopping . . . and Even Some Food Prep

If grocery shopping is among your least favorite things to do and you don't mind someone else shopping for you, opt for an online grocery shopping service such as Peapod.com. Some stores also offer an online ordering system so you can select your items in advance for pick up.

Shop with Your Kids

Taking kids with you to the grocery store is a double-edged sword. It takes longer. There's the prospect of meltdown and the clamoring for junk food. And the chasing of children. But grocery shopping with kids can also be an opportunity to educate your kids about nutrition, money, and independence while spending time together—and it can even be fun. Here are a few basic operating tips to keep your shopping trip running smoothly.

 At some point I decided to shift my perspective on grocery shopping and think of it as a fun activity with my kids. When I'm on my own with Violet, I look at grocery runs as a way to get out of the house and show her something new (if I just need a few items, I run with the jogging stroller and piggyback my own self-care). When I'm alone with Laurel, I use it as reconnection time. We chat, she serves as my helper, we enjoy some samples, and I usually offer her a treat (amazingly, she doesn't always take me up on it). I know a lot of parents are skeptical about the fun factor, but we really end up having a good time.

One rainy weekend afternoon, the girls and I were getting a little stir crazy so I suggested we take care of the grocery shopping.

Laurel resisted at first, as she tends to want to just hang out in her jammies all weekend long, but we eventually got out the door (I told her she could wear her jammies to the store, which she thought was *awesome*).

We ended up having a lovely time. It was one of Violet's first times sitting in the shopping cart and Laurel was so excited to push Vi around and show her the store. It was incredibly sweet, and we got a chore done without it feeling like a chore. Laurel said, "Mom, keep asking me if I want to go to the grocery store. I know I usually say no, but it's because I forget how fun it is."

Enlist Your Older Child As a Helper

Kids love having a little control. Put your child in charge of checking items off the grocery list, bagging fruit (it's okay if they pick one or two squishy items), turning on the peanut butter or coffee grinding machines, or tracking down items as you work your way through the store. Turn small jobs into a game that lets them sidestep boredom and temptation.

Encourage Them to Pick Something New

While in the produce section, ask your kids if there are any new vegetables or fruits they would like try. Offering your children autonomy to choose will help them get excited about eating whatever they select.

Breeze Past the Junk Food Aisles

Seriously. You'll avoid much wheedling and cajoling. Some stores even have "family friendly" checkout lines with fewer tabloids and candy bars.

Don't Let the Occasional Meltdown Deter You

Public meltdowns are maddening, but like anything in life, just because they happen once doesn't mean they'll happen every time. When kids grow up with the expectation of "grocery shopping manners," they will eventually fall in line. The learning and the time you'll have together are worth the wait.

Sourcing Local

Signing up for a community supported agriculture (CSA) share, stopping by a farmer's market, or growing a backyard garden may at some level feel like more work, but such choices may support your newly-minimalized meal plan in other ways. The key is to find a way to source local that works for you but is not driven by guilt.

We were devoted to our CSA share for two years. I loved the variety of produce and the fact that picking up our share created an opportunity to talk to Laurel about the food cycle. It also encouraged her to eat more vegetables. However, the pickup location and time were not convenient for us, particularly as a one-car family. It turned our CSA from a beloved partner to a chore we grew to resent.

I realized I was carrying a lot of guilt and "should" feelings about the CSA, and that I could easily solve this problem by continuing to source local food in different ways—whether by patronizing local farms via our grocery store (which highlights local produce) or by shopping at one of the weekly farmer's markets near our home.

Stefania Butler of citymama.typepad.com: The key to making the most out of the CSA delivery is to be sure that you process everything the day you get it. This means that each delivery day I spend about an hour washing and spin-drying greens, roasting or boiling root veggies, and chopping celery and carrots into sticks for lunches or dices for recipes throughout the week. It is so much easier to just grab already roasted beets and toss them into a salad (or grind into baby food with chicken and sweet potatoes) or toss prewashed spinach into a pan with olive oil and roasted garlic. Taking the time when you get your delivery will save you from throwing away unused produce a week later.

Food can be simple, nourishing, and fun. Aligning your family's food style and scheduling, meal planning, and adopting a few tricks to streamline grocery shopping will go a long way in helping you figure out your family's minimalized mealtime. Now it's time to get on to the food preparation and eating!

12

Simplifying and Enjoying Mealtime

The Norman Rockwell fantasy is a happy, animated family sitting around a beautifully set and stocked dinner table. It's a lovely image: there is something elementally nourishing about time spent sharing meals. But it's impossible to live up to such a standard day to day, even though the lifestyle magazines and cooking shows would have you believe otherwise.

Minimalizing your mealtime expectations by simplifying the preparation and presentation puts the focus back where it feels right: on the conversation and connection that happens during meals. But what if sitting down to eat together every night just isn't realistic? That's fine, too. The point is for eating to be a source of pleasure and nourishment, not guilt.

In this chapter, we share ways to streamline your meal preparation and to make mealtimes more fun.

Meal Preparation Made Easy

The simpler your meals, the simpler the preparation involved. These tips will speed up your cooking considerably.

Separate Ingredient Prep from Cooking

During weekdays, the realities of work, school, homework, and after-school activities means that there's less time to fuss over food prep. Depending on your menu plan, prep a few items over the weekend so it's easy to knock together meals quickly during the week. Chop vegetables, prepare and/or brown cuts of meat, and measure and assemble seasonings. You can even freeze prepped menu items for use throughout the week.

 Over the weekend, I like to prep one large container filled with a variety of chopped vegetables. Doing this makes it easier to snack well, and also to assemble salads and add veggies to pizzas, quesadillas, and other meals.

Make Your Most Involved Meal on the Weekend

If you're making something that requires a little more prep or a longer cooking time, make it on the weekend, when you have fewer time constraints. If you can, make a meal that will yield leftovers or lunches for later in the week.

Get Feedback but Don't Be a Short Order Cook

Much mealtime tension hinges on parents offering food and kids not wanting to eat it. You've already planned your meals; now *stay firm* about serving them. Your job is to provide a nutritious meal, not to force it down your child's throat or get up and down repeatedly to accommodate culinary changes of heart. Also, avoiding the role of short order cook will inspire your kids to help themselves if they truly need another option.

Eat Color

Meals are more appealing when they're colorful. Add quick color infusions with snap peas, carrot sticks, and cherry tomatoes. Include colorful fruit to brighten the plate, fill the belly, and satisfy the sweet tooth.

Find Ways to Boost the Nutrition in Family Favorites

Worry less about your family's specific food choices by bumping up the nutrition level in dishes they're already eating. We're not suggesting that you "hide" vegetables in brownies, but that you use familiar foods as an easy way to increase healthy food intake overall. For example, Christine adds a half block of crushed tofu to the sauce for her lasagna to bump up the protein content (perfect, since Laurel is a vegetarian).

Michelle Stern of whatscookingwithkids.com: For pasta dishes, I beef up the nutrients by using Barilla Plus pasta, which is partially made from garbanzo bean flour and adds protein to the otherwise carbohydrate-rich noodles.

Clear Your Fridge

Menu planning and list making will help minimize food waste. But inevitably you get to a point in the week when your fridge is full of random odds and ends. Cue the soups, enchiladas, and stir-fries!

My friends Anne and Michael live in London and introduced me to the term "butler's salad," which apparently refers to a salad comprised of pantry (or refrigerator) odds and ends. I love making butler's salad as a means to eat more greens *and* make use of random leftovers (e.g., remnants from the baby carrots bag, the last quarter of a cucumber, etc.). After starting with a base of lettuce and raw vegetables, I add nutrient-rich goodies such as nuts, leftover steak or chicken, hardboiled eggs, or (frozen then cooked) falafel. I top it with my favorite dressing or simply drizzle a little olive oil and balsamic vinegar, sprinkle coarse salt and pepper over the top, and I'm done. I've been known to eat these salads for lunch *and* dinner, sometimes several days in a row. I also use this method with a base of quinoa or brown rice.

Invest in Kitchen Gear to Simplify Cooking

There might be one or two purchases that would streamline your kitchen time enough to be worth the money and storage space. Busy weeknights might go more smoothly with a rice cooker or a slow cooker. Leftovers stay fresher and look more appetizing (and pantry chaos subsides) with a matching set of reusable containers. A good stock of sealable freezer bags and aluminum foil makes freezing ingredients and leftovers so much easier. Try to choose items that will simplify cooking *and* cleanup.

Involve Your Family in Meal Preparation

What if your partner or your kids were responsible for preparing one or more meals per week? Think of the life skills and the fun to be had! Okay, perhaps, in the beginning, the fun will mostly be yours, but it's worth a conversation, especially if the meal is simple and popular (such as pasta, salad, and garlic bread). Here are some tips for getting your family involved in the kitchen:

Let Go of Perfection

A big part of engaging kids in the kitchen involves letting go of perfection. The chopped veggies do not need to be uniform. If your child wants to make crazy shapes with the cookie dough, why not? When you let your kid take charge (within reason) you'll be amazed by how focused he'll get on the project and the result.

Give Age-Appropriate Tasks

Obviously, age will determine how much your child can do, but when your toddler can follow simple instructions, she will love dumping premeasured ingredients in a bowl. Older kids can measure and mix, help assemble (e.g., pizza), and prep ingredients.

Be Clear About Safety

You will want to supervise kitchen work, particularly as your child gets old enough to wield a knife or turn on the stove. Offer her frequent reminders about safety to start, and she will get the hang of it.

Encourage Autonomy

As your kid grows more confident in the kitchen, encourage his autonomy. It may lead somewhere amazing.

 I love cooking and baking so I brought Laurel into the kitchen with me early on. When she was a toddler she enjoyed dumping in and mixing ingredients. As a preschooler she started to measure and assemble. When she was five years old she started chopping soft foods with a Zyliss plastic knife. About a year later she became adept (with our repeated warnings and supervision with each use) with a paring knife. At seven years old she could bake a chocolate cake from scratch and pipe the frosting impressively.

I found that Laurel's excitement and focus on cooking projects really took off when I let go and simply encouraged her to do it her way. I told her to not worry about cutting vegetables into perfectly uniform dice (though I did explain the concept that smaller items cook faster than larger ones). I let her sculpt dough scraps into whatever embellishments she wanted on top of the Thanksgiving apple pie. I encouraged her to decorate the pizza in whatever way she wanted, whether that involved random clusters of vegetables, stripes, or something else.

One afternoon Laurel (then five years old) stopped me as I was about to make dinner and said, "Mommy, just go and sit and relax on the couch while I make dinner." I had been planning on making tofu and vegetable soup and she declared that she would make it. Plus sandwiches.

I cut a couple of harder to manage items (onion, potato) and she cut the tofu, mushrooms, and zucchini with her Zyliss. I set her up at the stove (at this point she was definitely heat element aware) and off she went...tossing in olive oil in "cute blobs" and adding in ingredients. I relaxed on the couch with a magazine and one ear out.

As she was finishing, Laurel and I set the table together and then she, Jon, and I sat down as a family. I am convinced that the soup and sandwiches tasted better by her hand.

Try Planting a Vegetable Garden

Whether you have space for a large assortment of veggies, have only a small area for planting, or confine your efforts to a pot of herbs or a bowl of lettuce growing on the kitchen table, working/playing in the garden with kids is fun and educational. And, as often happens when kids have input into the process, they are much more likely to try produce that they have planted and helped grow.

Bringing Joy Back to Mealtime

Time to eat! The planning work you've done to simplify shopping and cooking will hopefully leave you with more energy and spirit to enjoy your meal. You deserve more than basic sustenance when you sit down to the table: you deserve appreciation, time to connect with your family, and the satisfaction of a job well done.

Set an End to Snack Time

Nothing's more frustrating than serving a meal to people who aren't hungry. Close the snack train at least an hour before dinnertime.

Set the Table for Easy Cleanup

Now's the time to let go of the magazine standard definition of what a weeknight dinner table should look like. Plates, napkins, cutlery, and glasses—that's all you need. Save the fussy placemats and accessories for weekends and guests. That said, if you enjoy dressing up the table, simple touches like some flowers or greenery picked from the garden and perched in a glass jar can do wonders.

If your kids are old enough, table setting is an ideal task to delegate. Asha's kids are responsible for setting the table after they're done with homework, and before they head off for before-dinner free time.

Start with a Moment of Gratitude

When everyone's tired and famished and still likely mentally transitioning from a busy day of work and school, there's a tendency to strap on the feedbag and go, as it were. But it's worth slowing down and starting each meal with an expression of gratitude—whether it's for one another, the food, the cook, or something else. In general, treating mealtime less like a refueling break and more like a ritual can effectively transform the mood and pace of dinner.

Limit the Up and Down

One thing that can contribute to a frenetic-feeling meal is constant getting up from the table. Make a family rule about not getting up unless it's truly necessary and try doing without whatever you forgot to bring to the table. Or wait until you've thought of more than one thing you've forgotten so you make fewer trips. As with the moment of gratitude, this is a small but meaningful tweak that will calm the mealtime atmosphere.

Do a Round of Updates

Encourage everyone to share something from his or her day, whether it was something fun, exciting, or frustrating. Getting in the habit of open sharing will help establish mealtimes as safe opportunities for family communication.

Up the Fun Quotient

There are so many ways to inject a little levity into family mealtime. Have everyone tell a joke. Spread out a blanket and have a picnic on the floor. Even changing seating positions can change the mood.

Insist on Respect for the Cook

You're bound to bring a meal to the table that your family's not clamoring to eat. That's fine—there's no way you can please every palate every time. But you can make a rule that groans, eye rolls, and complaints are not allowed. A simple "no, thank you" will suffice.

Manners Matter

You'd be surprised by what a little attention to manners can do. When you're not busy asking people to stop burping, slurping, and interrupting, you can relax and enjoy the good food and conversation. This gets easier as kids get older, of course, so think of it as a gradual process.

Everyone Cleans Up

Asha discovered that her major mealtime downer was the post-meal scatter. After she'd spent time cooking, having to also clear the table and clean up the kitchen was a source of major resentment... which usually came out later in the evening. Agree on family-wide cleanup so that your kids learn that everyone shares in the joy *and* the work of mealtime.

Easy Breakfasts and Lunches

We've focused on dinner in this chapter because it's the meal that benefits most from planning and forethought. But there are two other meals per day people are eating... plus snacks. The good news is that these meals are much easier to simplify.

At Home

Eating at home should be easy and nourishing. It's where you can best encourage your child's autonomy, and keep things simple with routines, leftovers, and a well-stocked freezer.

Limit Breakfast and Lunch Options

Breakfast and lunch are two meals that lend themselves to repetition. Asha has oatmeal and coffee for breakfast every morning, and her kids have cold cereal. No need to hold yourself to the same expectations of variety you do for dinner.

Encourage Kids to Prepare Their Own Meals

Place breakfast and lunch utensils at kid-height so they can serve themselves. Same with the milk and other ingredients in the pantry and refrigerator. Show kids how to make sandwiches. Wash fruit and keep it in a bowl on the table so they can grab and go.

Take Advantage of Leftovers

Leftovers inspire strong feelings: either you love them (Asha regularly raids her friends' refrigerators for their leftovers) or you don't. If you're not a fan of leftovers, open your mind to using them as an already prepared component of a new meal. Chili can be wrapped in a tortilla. Leftover stir-fries can be tossed with dressing as a salad or folded into an omelet. Random odds and ends can go into a butler's salad (see Christine's description earlier in the chapter).

Take Advantage of Your Freezer

Pancakes, waffles, bread, shredded cheese, and other healthy prepared foods can live in the freezer. All they need is a quick toast or thaw and they're ready to eat.

At School

Many parents dread packing lunch. And sometimes there's just no respite (for example, if your daughter is like Laurel and doesn't want to wait on the cafeteria line because the lunch period is already so rushed). Here are some ways to streamline the process:

Lower Your Expectations

Again, no need for huge variety here. A meal balanced with protein, a fruit, a vegetable, and a grain, plus water to drink is fine, but if you don't cover all the nutritional bases every single day, that's okay too. Do your best to balance out your child's food choices at home throughout the week.

Quiz Your Kid for Ideas

Sometimes, the hardest thing about packing lunch is knowing what to pack. Ask your kid to do a little reconnaissance at lunchtime: What are other kids eating that looks good? This is how Asha found out that Mira wanted to try egg salad. She had tried her friend's sandwich and loved it!

Prep Lunches Ahead of Time

Lunch making is less stressful in the mornings when some of the pieces are already in place. On Mondays and Wednesdays Christine packs Laurel's fruit and vegetable containers and sets aside snack options (e.g., yogurt, granola bars) for two days. The main course (e.g., sandwich, macaroni and cheese, soup, etc.) gets made fresh the morning of school, depending on what Laurel is in the mood for.

Stefania Butler of citymama.typepad.com: I pack lunch at the dinner table the night before! Before I clean up dinner, I pack anything left over into bento boxes for lunch the next day.

Get in a Rhythm with Reusable Containers

Reusable containers are great to help you and your kids get in a rhythm with lunch prep and cleanup. Asha packs her kids' lunch boxes with small, disposable plastic containers that her kids load in the dishwasher when they get home.

Michelle Stern of whatscookingwithkids.com: We always use reusable containers or lunchboxes with compartments for each food item—this way, I simply pack one of each of the following items into each compartment: a fruit, a veggie, a crunchy snack, and something with protein.

Let Your Kid Take Over the Job

If you truly hate packing your kid's lunch, work toward handing over the job. Prep lunch items in the fridge over the weekend, and have your child assemble her lunch each morning before school. Laurel's lunch-making skills have even inspired her to pack her parents a lunch every now and then!

Snack Strategies

Snacks are tricky. They're an important part of a kid's nutritional day, but they lend themselves to unhealthy habits such as eating for entertainment. Following are a few ideas for keeping snack time easy and healthy.

Lower the Intensity Around Forbidden Foods

We all want our kids to eat food that supports their health and growth. But surrounding food with an atmosphere of tension sabotages that goal in the long run. Offer the healthy stuff, and allow for treats in moderation as well. By lowering the intensity around "forbidden" foods, you lessen their attractiveness.

 Growing up, we rarely had junk food in the house—not because my parents were morally opposed to it, but because it was considered a wasteful expense. As a result, my siblings and I went *crazy* over junk food whenever we had the chance. I often used my lunch money entirely on desserts from the school lunch line (come to think of it, the lunch ladies never gave me a hard time about this) or, I'd stop at the convenience store on the way to school and spend my lunch money entirely on candy (at one point my mom got wind of this and actually called the store and told them to stop selling to me...how embarrassing). I also will admit that being deprived of sweets led me to a phase of shoplifting Swedish fish from the local five and dime. To this day, my stomach (and conscience) feels sick when I think about Swedish fish.

We've taken a different approach with Laurel. Treats are around, and we encourage moderation and stopping once satisfied. Laurel enjoys sweets as much as the next kid, but she's able to make decisions about sugar based on whether she actually wants it versus just eating it because it is there.

Make the Healthy Stuff Easy to Grab

If your kids are going to snack on healthy foods, they need to be as easy to grab as the bag of chips. Good candidates include single servings of precut vegetables and fruit, string cheese, yogurt, whole grain crackers, and nuts. Asha portions nuts, crackers, and pretzels into plastic cups so her kids can grab them *and* they get an education about portion sizes.

Use Snacks As a Way to Even Out the Day's Nutrition

If your kids routinely avoid the fruits and vegetables in their meals, set out an attractive platter of fruits and vegetables during snack time. You'd be amazed by what kids are willing to eat when they're grazing between activities as opposed to sitting at the dinner table.

On weekends when we eat brunch in the late morning and don't quite have the appetite for a full lunch in advance of dinner, we go for a nice assembly of snacks in the afternoon. I recently set Laurel up with a great project that was fun for her to do and encouraged well-rounded snacking: I gave her a twelve-cup muffin tin and suggested she fill it with twelve snacks. She canvassed the fridge and cupboard and filled the cups with fruits and veggies she cut up (e.g., watermelon, strawberries, blueberries, carrots, cucumber, bell peppers) as well as pantry snacks (e.g., graham sticks, dried dates, small crackers, cereal). It was the perfect between-meal grazing platform and a fun activity as well.

Feeding Babies and Toddlers

If you have very small people at home, it'll be a while before they're helping in the kitchen and enjoying your well-planned meals. Even so, many of the principles around minimalizing your mealtime apply. That said, here are our thoughts on feeding babies and toddlers.

The Milk Months

The choice to breastfeed or formula feed your baby is yours. This is a good moment to repeat a key of Minimalist Parenting: *know yourself.* Do what works for you and do not beat yourself up comparing yourself to others. Truly. Repeat that again and again if you're doubting yourself, as many new mothers do when navigating this choice. Every mother's situation is different and complex. However you ultimately feed your baby, you are nourishing your child. You have many, many years and meals ahead of you, all of which will contribute to your kid's growth.

 Jules Pieri of DailyGrommet.com, via PopDiscourse.com: I loved breastfeeding my three sons far more than I had ever imagined and did so for nine months at the shortest and thirteen months at the longest. Here is the funny thing…I can't remember how long for which one. It mattered A LOT at the time. It does not matter one iota a couple years down the road…Family happiness is family happiness and that includes you being able to provide for your family and your own well-being.

The Solid Food Adventure

It can be both exciting and a little stressful when you introduce solid food to your baby. Here are a few thoughts to keep in mind:

Follow, but Try Not to Worry About, the Schedules
There are plenty of guides that tell you which foods to introduce when. In general, the party line is to introduce a new food for three days before trying another new one so you can monitor for allergic reactions.

Getting into this three-day new food cycle can leave new parents fretting over checking off each item on the list. We say it's fine to take it at your own pace—if you feed baby the same collection of solid foods for a week, no problem. There's no time limit on introducing new foods.

Embrace the Mess

Feeding babies can be messy, especially when they start developing the dexterity to pick up food bits and mash them all over their faces. Instead of trying to control the mess (which is inevitable), let them explore. It's sensory fun for them, and may occupy them for a bit of time so you can actually eat too. Besides, you'll need to change their clothes and wipe them down anyway.

Healthy Food Is Healthy Food, Regardless of the Source

Some people (like Christine) actually enjoy making baby food, but if you find this a tiresome chore, buy prepared baby food and don't look back. There are so many great options (including several major organic lines) to choose from.

As Soon As Your Child Is Interested, Feed Her from Your Plate

Rejoice when your toddler is ready to eat table food. Less preparation—yay! Early on Christine found that Violet was very excited about trying bits of whatever everyone else was eating—whether it was steel-cut oats at breakfast or bits of vegetarian chili or lasagna at dinner.

Encourage Mealtime Independence

We discussed embracing mess earlier, and this is a big part of encouraging mealtime independence. You want your kids to become explorers in all aspects of life—this is what will help them become independent and, equally important, frees up *your* hands. Let your baby use his hands to play with his food, and then put baby utensils on his tray and let him play with them and figure out how to use them.

 We once visited friends who have four kids. The mom looked at Laurel—who was younger than my friend's twin girls but was zipping her own coat (which the twins could not do)—and said, "Wow, we're usually so focused on getting from point A to B that we help the kids get their shoes on and zip up their jackets. This is reminding me that I should teach the kids to zip their zippers and tie their shoes so I don't have to do it!"

I felt the same way with Violet when she was a new solid food eater. I was so fixed on getting her to eat I forgot to let her just do it herself. I saw a friend (whose baby is about the same age) post Facebook pictures of her son using a fork and I thought, "Wow, I totally forgot about introducing utensils because I've been focused on getting the food in!" I started placing a spoon and fork on Violet's tray and very quickly, she figured out how to use them to feed herself. Cue angels singing.

The wonderful thing about minimalizing meal preparation is that it gives you the space to actually enjoy what you're eating (and with whom you're eating). As you go about feeding your family, keep in mind that every meal does not need to be nutritionally perfect, or even good tasting (some of the best family stories come from meals gone awry). Instead, focus on a general healthy plan, allow treats in moderation, and ignore your harshest critic (you!).

TOP TIME- AND EFFORT-SAVING TIPS

Food is a big part of family life but it need not consume your entire day! We asked Aviva Goldfarb of The Six O'clock Scramble (thescramble.com) for her favorite time and effort saving kitchen tips:

- **Make sure you have good-quality knives and keep them sharpened.** A good pair of kitchen scissors can also make easier work of cutting herbs, scallions, and other foods.
- **Organize your kitchen.** If you know where the vegetables are in your refrigerator (I keep one drawer for fruit and one for veggies), and can quickly lay your hands on the black beans and bowtie noodles, dinner prep will go a lot faster.
- **Before you begin to cook, clear off the kitchen counters**, empty the dishwasher (or delegate this task to another family member), and pull out all

of the ingredients. These steps make dinner preparation a lot less chaotic and make it go faster.

- **As you're cooking, collect all your trash in a small container by the sink** rather than going back and forth to the kitchen trashcan. You can empty it out when you're done cooking (preferably into a compost bin!).
- **Do food prep in advance for meals and lunches.** Before you clean up from Tuesday evening's dinner, chop up the onion and the peppers that you'll need for Wednesday's dinner and when you're cutting up carrots for tomorrow's lunch, cut enough for the whole week. You'll want to kiss yourself tomorrow!
- **Get a head start during the day.** While the kids are eating breakfast or doing homework, or while you are on a long call, wash and/or chop the vegetables you'll need, and pull out the pots and pans and nonperishable ingredients you'll need later.
- **Put the ingredients away as you use them, so cleanup goes more quickly.** When you are ready to do the dishes, stack all of the dirty dishes by the sink and load the dishwasher first (most dishes don't need to be rinsed), so your dishwashing goes quickly and you use less water.

13

Celebrations and Vacations: Less Fuss, More Fun

Acornerstone philosophy of Minimalist Parenting—make room for remarkable—sums up our approach to celebrations, holidays and travel. Too often, minimalism is associated with scarcity, utilitarianism, and a tendency to shun the big splurge. But we take a different slant: fun and togetherness is the whole point! One of the most important gifts you can give your family is a mental album full of happy memories. In a few years, those memories will be worth more to you than a clean house or a thousand more dollars.

When you clear away the clutter and stress in your family life, you open up opportunities for recreation and celebration. Just think: the time and money you save by minimalizing can be spent on a vacation or another memory-making occasion. Bring on the joy!

While we believe in regular investments in family fun, we also know that special occasions can turn into black holes of excess and expectation. Who hasn't attended an over-the-top birthday party or felt inadequate when faced with a neighbor's perfectly decorated Christmas tree? In this chapter, we've got plenty of ideas for bringing parties, holidays, and travel back to earth and keeping the focus on what matters: the joy and deepened relationships these occasions are meant to inspire.

Birthday Parties

Making fun of the reality TV show *Outrageous Kid Parties* is easy pickings; intellectually, most of us agree that simple birthday parties are the way to go. But keeping the party budget in check is only part of the picture. If party preparation, planning, and management exhaust you to the point of resentment, it's time to change the formula. Here are some steps you can take to simplify birthday celebrations.

Plan a Party That Works for You and Your Kid

Before you buy a single birthday candle, give some thought to what would be fun for both you and your kid. Granted, your kid is the guest of honor so his preferences are an important part of making the occasion special and memorable, but you—clearly—are the one doing the heavy lifting.

Be Honest About Your Motivations

Getting to the heart of your motivations around celebrations will help you identify your party priorities. You may be surprised to find that your expectations have more to do with your needs than your child's. Ask yourself:

- Am I doing this because I love throwing parties and (perhaps a little) showing off my entertaining skills?
- Am I compensating for something missing from my own childhood?
- Am I doing this because everyone else is throwing large parties and inviting the entire class?

Birthdays typically have been a bit of a sensitive spot for me. Growing up, my siblings and I never had "friend" birthdays parties, partly because our family of nine (or sometimes more, depending on which relatives were bunking with us) provided enough of a crowd, partly because our house tended to be in a state of disrepair, and partly because birthday parties including lots of other kids were an added expense that was understandably challenging for my parents.

I was acutely aware of all these things as a small person, but I still longed for birthday parties with lots of friends, both because I felt bad about attending other kids' parties and not reciprocating, and because I grew up with a bit of a complex about friends. I was different racially and socioeconomically from most of my peers, and I craved their acceptance and friendship.

As a result, Laurel's birthdays were very important to me. I wanted to celebrate her. Surround her with friends and family. Show her she was loved. For her first three birthdays I threw big parties—not lavish or outrageous thematically, but given that we have a large family and many friends with kids nearby, the gatherings tended to be at least thirty to forty people.

I would exhaust myself making tons of food and giant cakes. (I do love baking and probably was showing off a little here.) And Laurel? In the face of such large gatherings, she would bury her face in my shoulder and look apprehensive, even among beloved family and friends. I finally came to terms with my motivations because they were clearly so out of joint with Laurel's temperament.

Tailor Party Plans to Your Child's Temperament

Once you're clear about your own motivations, you'll be able to see clearly what's most important: what your kid would enjoy.

Starting with Laurel's fourth birthday, I decided to take things down several notches. I incorporated Laurel in the decision making and we hosted small, simple parties. She was happy. We were happy. I couldn't believe I hadn't done this earlier! On her sixth birthday, our oven was broken so I couldn't bake a cake. I bought a delicious cake and, as much as I love baking, couldn't believe I had never "outsourced" cake before. Huge timesaver.

When Violet's first birthday rolled around, my mind-set was totally different. Part of it likely had to do with the natural relaxation of standards that happens with second children, but I also felt as if I had grown and learned so much from our experience with Laurel. We hosted a small, simple gathering with just immediate family, where all I did in advance was cut up fruit salad, make a cake (not over the top but pretty), and hang a few simple decorations.

It was perfectly celebratory—and ironically, very much like the parties of my childhood.

Consider Throwing Parties Every Few Years

Everyone should feel special on her birthday, but there's no rule that says your kid has to have an elaborate party every year. Family gatherings, simple traditions, sleepovers, or a day out with one or two good friends can be just as special as a big party, especially if (as for Laurel) big parties are overwhelming.

Plan Separate Celebrations

If you have a large family, consider planning two separate (but simple!) gatherings to keep the numbers more intimate. One year, Christine planned Laurel's friend and family parties over the same weekend—she kept the time windows short so it wouldn't feel like the whole weekend was consumed by party prep, execution, and cleanup. She found that, because the parties were close together, she could plan for and prepare the same refreshments and leave the same decorations up for both parties.

 Erin via the Minimalist Parenting blog: One tip I learned from my sister in-law about birthdays—we only do ONE cake. So if my son's actual birthday is on a Tuesday, but his friend party is the following Saturday, his one and only cake will be with his friends on Saturday. We will stick candles in the breakfast pancakes (or whatever he's requested). I can't believe I went so many years making TWO cakes!

Play to Your Strengths

If you're a natural party planner, wonderful! Planning your kids' birthday parties is likely a source of joy, and you should run with it! But if you're not one for entertaining, the idea of hosting twelve five-year-olds in your house may fill you with dread. No need to feel guilty—just ask for help.

Mira loves to swim and is in her element in the pool. I'm not a confident swimmer, and I'm perfectly happy dangling my feet in the water. When Mira asked to host her birthday party at the community pool, I cringed inside. The idea of supervising multiple beginning swimmers got my anxiety meter rising. But it had been a couple of years since Mira had had a big party, so I decided to go for it.

Rael is a fantastic swimmer, so I delegated the job of in-pool grown-up to him. I also bucked the usual drop-off protocol and asked the parents of emerging swimmers to wear their swimsuits and stay to assist. I'm sure more than one parent groaned at the thought, but I decided to stick to my limits. If I had jumped into the pool to supervise while also trying to handle the cake, presents, and other party activities, my resentment and anxiety would have brought down the entire party. In the end, everyone had a great time, including the parents who stayed to swim.

Outsource It

If you want to save on the prep/mess factor at home, another great solution is to outsource the party. No need for an expensive, chaotic trip to the local pizza-arcade-party factory! Consider these great ideas:

Carla via BostonMamas.com: Our girls have birthdays in October and June, and we do the same thing every year, for every birthday. We invite all of our friends and family to meet us at the local park. We bring juice boxes, bottled water, fruit salad, and mini cupcakes, and the pizza is delivered. The kids have a great time running around outside, the adults get to talk, and we don't have to clean up a house afterward. It's super easy and a lot of fun!

Aisha via BostonMamas.com: I have four children and after the first I learned quickly about the "less is more" concept. Now every year I ask them what they want to do and we make it just an immediate family affair. For my son Thaison's eighth birthday, we asked him what he wanted and he said anything science. We will have dinner at a restaurant of his choice (so long as it isn't too expensive) then we are surprising him with a trip to a science museum. He has never been so I am definitely excited to see his reaction!

Host an Open Neighborhood Party

If you have the benefit of living in a neighborhood with lots of kids, throw a party just for them.

Lynn via BostonMamas.com: Here on our block in Chicago the parents came up with "neighbor birthdays." We put out a flyer with the date and time, and kids and parents come over to the front yard of the birthday kid's house for cake. We take a group picture on the porch steps and call it a day. The whole thing takes about an hour, there are no (or very small) gifts, the parents get to visit, and the kids of all ages have fun. We have a wonderful record of the children growing up with the porch step photographs. All of the neighbors have done this for about twenty years.

Minimalist Birthday Party Tips

Once you've decided on the type of party you're going to host, there are easy ways to simplify each aspect of the party itself.

Decide on a Reasonable Number of Guests

A common rule of thumb is one person per year of the child's age. But once kids start school, that's not always possible as class-wide parties become the norm. If you don't have the energy to host a class-wide party, that's perfectly fine. Simply distribute invitations outside of school and to talk to your child about the importance of discretion.

Simplify Invitations

Printed or hand-lettered invitations are lovely—but only if you and your child enjoy making them. For everyone else, electronic invites via e-mail, Evite, or Paperless Post are quick, easy, and get the job done.

Ask for RSVPs, but Don't Worry About Stragglers

It's always handy to know how many people are going to show up at your party, especially when guests arrive with siblings. But a few RSVPs are bound to get lost in the parenting chaos. Plan on a few extra portions of food and don't worry about it.

Set an End Time

Always err on the side of a shorter party, and note a specific end time on the invitation. As kids get older, most parents will expect to drop off their kids and pick them up at the end of the party. If you'd like some grown up assistants, be sure to arrange for them ahead of time.

Reduce the Expectations About Meals

A party doesn't necessarily have to involve a meal. A selection of self-serve snacks and drinks, plus birthday cake, make for a perfectly festive food setup. If you set your party time between lunch and dinner, the expectations will be clear.

Simplify the Decor

It's amazing how far a few balloons, streamers, or tissue paper balls go toward creating a festive atmosphere. In fact, to create a cohesive and festive party atmosphere in mere minutes, pick up plates, napkins, a disposable tablecloth, and balloons in the same color palette and you're good to go.

Prioritize Tasks in Order of Fun Factor—Then Let the Rest Go

Even when your plans are simple, sometimes the tasks can still stack up. Prioritize the things that bring you the most joy and let go of the rest.

 Laurel, like me, has a tendency to make plans. And despite the fact that our plans for Violet's first birthday party were quite simple, a couple of days before the party, Laurel actually said, "I'm getting stressed about all of the things I want to do!" At which point, I suggested we sit down and list the things we both wanted to do and number them in order of most to least fun…and to not worry about letting stuff at the bottom of the list go.

It ended up being a really fun and illuminating exercise. We realized that baking was top on the list for both of us (me: cake, her: cookies). We also ended up letting several items at the bottom of the list go— including extra errands such as buying potted violets for my family to take home. We just didn't bother and instead sent everyone home with extra cake and cookies…perfect! And it felt *fantastic*.

Skip the Goodie Bags!

There! We said it! We love the generous spirit behind goodie bags and party favors, but we could all do without random tchotchkes that get played with for five seconds (if that) and then stuffed in a drawer. How about hosting a simple craft activity and letting the result serve as the parting gift? Or sending kids home with something edible/usable? Or taking a group photo and printing out copies (at the party or after) for each child to keep?

One year, we used Frisbees as trays to serve the paper plates full of birthday cake. At the end of the party, each guest had a Frisbee to take home and play with for the rest of the summer. Another year we gave out binder-pouches stuffed with school supplies picked up on super-clearance. The parents *and* the kids loved them.

Team Up with a Friend

Does your child have a good buddy with a birthday in close proximity? Team up to reduce effort (and scheduling) for all!

When Laurel was in preschool, she and her good friend Grace had birthdays about a week apart and shared the same circle of friends. So Grace's mom and I decided to celebrate their friendship with a joint birthday party.

The girls loved the idea, the parents were psyched to be able to celebrate the girls *and* have one less thing on the calendar, and the joint party was a fantastic way to lighten the load for each family, as we split up all the party duties. Because this was basically a playdate birthday party—we didn't have a specific craft that would result in a takeaway item for a party favor—I ordered cookies with a photo of the two birthday girls printed in icing. Cute, edible, and tchotchke-free!

Graduation and Other Milestone Markers

Rites of passage are wonderful hallmarks of childhood. Graduations, bar mitzvahs, and even sweet sixteen birthdays—each occasion has special significance, depending upon your background or history. But when *every* transition becomes the basis of a party, the specialness starts to fade.

We're not suggesting you withhold your natural expressions of pride that come out when your kid makes it to the end of a school year, sports season, or particularly challenging assignment. Those pats on the back are incredibly important. But they tend to be drowned out in the glare of a big, shiny party. Kids get distracted by the gifts and treats and miss noticing the true satisfaction that comes with their accomplishment.

We'd like to issue a minimalist call for keeping special milestones truly sacred. Graduation from high school? A big deal worthy of celebration and recognition. Graduation from second grade? Not so much. If anything, hugs and milkshakes on the last day of school are more than enough. Summer is the ultimate reward!

Holidays

Oh, the holidays. They're supposed to be fun and meaningful, and yet for so many families holidays become a time of chaos and oversized expectations. The food, the decorations, the family dynamics, the time/money pressures…everything gets compressed into a single day (or season) of stress.

But let's step back for a moment to consider common holiday stressors:

- Too many party invitations
- Subpar decorations
- Last-minute shopping

- Cooking the "right" food and serving it on a perfectly set table
- Proper attire, whether it's a homemade costume or the perfect party dress
- Family expectations
- Budget constraints
- Too many houseguests
- Worry that the holiday won't feel "special" enough unless it's celebrated with all the trappings

Are these "problems" really worthy of your stress? (Repeat after us: "No.")

Minimalizing the holidays will bring back the joy, no matter what your background or tradition. It *is* possible to transform holiday burdens into memorable occasions, whether they are neighborhood Halloween festivities, a food- and football-filled Thanksgiving, or a relaxed Christmas (yes, such a thing exists).

Make a Plan, Then Edit It

Map out a plan that contains the *minimum* amount of preparation that would make your holiday feel special. List gift recipients (we cover presents in the next section), menus, neighborhood events, travel plans, and anything else that goes into your holiday planning. Not only can you see the scope of your planning needs before you even start, but you also can prevent "holiday project creep" (randomly adding more things to your to-do list as you go).

Now look at the completed list. Are you feeling a growing sense of panic? Time to edit the list. Ruthlessly cross off the unnecessary or annoying. For example: if turning on the holiday house lights is a beloved kickoff for the season, keep it on the list. But if it's a curse-inducing headache, strike it. Same with homemade Halloween costumes. If fun, keep. If tiresome, toss.

Stick to Traditions

Creating and sticking to your own family traditions has logistical *and* emotional benefits.

Kristin Brandt of ManicMommies.com, via BostonMamas.com: I always set up our crèche in the front foyer, the tree in the "solarium" (a fancy way of describing our back room), and the Santa figures on the map drawer. We have Swedish meatballs for Christmas Eve dinner, cinnamon rolls for breakfast, and Paula Deen's foolproof standing prime rib roast for dinner. It's not that I don't want to try something new, it's that traditions such as these keep things easy and reduce the stress. And, they become something regular and anticipated for the kids.

We celebrate Hanukkah, and the traditional meal includes latkes (fried potato pancakes). Every time I forget about the latkes or skip them because I still don't have a great recipe, my kids miss them. One year I bought frozen latkes and heated them up in the oven. My husband and I could tell the difference, but my kids enjoyed them just as much as the homemade version. In the end, just *having* latkes made Hanukkah more special.

Embrace Imperfect

You know those holiday magazine spreads that make your decor and food look a little (okay, a lot) lackluster? Keep in mind that those spreads took hours to set up and shoot. By *teams of professionals*. Imperfect is okay. In fact, it's more than okay. It's what makes holiday moments real and fun and memorable. Garnish everything with parsley and call it done.

Despite my less-than-stellar craftiness, I enjoy making Halloween costumes for my kids. My big secret? I don't sew, and I view costumes more as interpretations than faithful representations. The whole thing comes together in collaboration with the kids. We use secondhand clothes, items from the dress-up box, a hot glue gun, safety pins, and duct tape. One year my daughter's "space boots" were sneakers covered in aluminum foil. The only reason it works is because we have so much fun doing it.

Rethink Hosting

If you love throwing parties but tend to exhaust yourself doing it, rethink your expectations about hosting. Either take a break from it completely and enjoy attending other people's gatherings, or simplify the food and preparations (or do a potluck!) to reduce stress and expense. The point is to enjoy time with your guests, not to be stuck working in the kitchen or panicking in the bathroom. People want to see you, not how perfectly you can assemble hors d'oeuvres.

Let Your Kids Help

Kids love the holidays, so why not get them involved? After all, doesn't the cuteness and heartfelt-ness of a present wrapped by a child outweigh the fact that the wrapping paper seams don't line up? Have your kids take the lead on decorations by finding holiday craft projects that will be fun, serve as decoration, and keep them busy while you take care of other preparations. The kids can also help with food gift assembly and cooking.

Pay Attention to Joy, Not Comparison

It's hard not to make comparisons around the holidays, but really, why? You will be a lot happier if you march to the beat of your own drummer. Not only will you relax about your own festivities, you'll be able to more fully appreciate others'.

 One holiday season, we received our first holiday card mere days after Thanksgiving and I immediately freaked out, lamenting that the cards had already started to arrive and that mine would be late (I felt extra guilty since I am a graphic designer). As I stood there, trying to mentally go through my work flow and figure out if I had time to design cards that week, Jon asked, "Why don't you just embrace and enjoy the greeting instead of looking at it as a symbol of any shortcomings?"

That comment really stuck with me. The whole point of holiday greetings is to reconnect, not race to the finish line. So that year we ended up sending our holiday cards in March (as spring greetings)— they were sent at a pace that worked for us and with heartfelt intentions and well wishes. And you know what? People went crazy over them because they loved receiving personal mail outside the holiday season.

Keep Travel Manageable

If your extended family lives far away, try to focus on travel arrangements that make the most sense for you and your family, *not* based on what will please everyone else. Ruffled feathers are not a reason to drain your bank account and your reserve of energy and goodwill during the holidays. Consider establishing an "every other year" tradition if holiday visits require long or expensive travel.

Accept That Family Dynamics Are Part of the Package

Family dynamics can be really tough, especially during the holidays. We all wish for happy, perfect relationships with extended family, but sometimes, old issues will come to the surface. Try to remember that your family is a work in progress, and that you can only control your own actions and reactions.

 All families seem to experience stress during the holidays, but the basic mathematical reality in my family is that its sheer size increases the likelihood of dissonance. My therapist shared a concept that has helped me enormously in many areas of my life: that I may not agree with how someone behaves, but it is not my job (in fact, I couldn't make it my job if I wanted to) to change that person. Instead, the best I can do is to figure out how to modify my own reaction to reduce/eliminate stress.

I've really taken this mantra to heart. With one fractured relationship in particular, I simply do my best to project forgiveness and healing in that direction and accept that our relationship is what it is in this moment. I can't control it so I just need to move on and focus on the relationships that are nourishing, not depleting.

Be Kind to Yourself

You and your family deserve this time to rejoice. You have worked hard all year—in your jobs, in your homes, raising your kids—and you deserve a break. Go only to those parties filled with the people you want to see, and politely decline the rest. Keep the decor and the food simple, and let the company make the season special. Do those things—and only those things—that make the holidays happy for you and your family. Then sit back and relax with some eggnog.

Minimalist Gift Giving: Setting Limits on Presents, Not Generosity

Minimalist parents love to give and receive gifts! But giving presents to every office mate, school staff member, niece or nephew, and neighbor? Not necessary. We've got suggestions for making gift giving manageable while still expressing your love and generosity.

Make a Plan and a Budget

During the holidays especially, gift buying can get out of hand. Make a gift list and budget in advance, using the aforementioned "make a holiday plan and edit it down" tactic. Nix the "shoulds" on the list. On the budgeting front, consider using the cash-in-envelope budgeting approach that Jessica shared in chapter 6 to help you avoid gift price creep.

Scale It Back

If you have a large family, set some parameters. When kids started to come into the mix, Christine and her siblings decided to stop exchanging gifts, instead focusing on time together. Small token gifts (e.g., homemade items) were optional, and wrapped gifts were reserved for the wee generation and the older generation (a sign of respect in Korean culture). That single decision reduced holiday stress and expense for the entire family.

Gift Usable Items

You simply can't go wrong with a usable gift, whether it's a coffee mug painted lovingly by your child or homemade treats such as spice rubs, cookie mix jars, or baked goods.

Use What You Already Have

Do you have an avid artist in your home? Turn artwork into gifts (make it classy by tossing it into an inexpensive frame). Another idea: assemble a series of artwork in a stack, punch two or three holes along one side, and fasten with ribbon for a beautiful, heartfelt art book. Your family will love these tokens, and it also tidies up your house by moving some of the artwork out.

Give Experiential Gifts

Whether it's tickets to a show, a museum membership, or a sleepover with a beloved relative, experiential gifts are clutter-free and offer an opportunity for bonding and creating lasting memories. These experiences need not be expensive, particularly for little ones with a limited attention span. Look into inexpensive performances by your local high school, college, church, or community arts group. If a family member asks what they can give your child, the gift of time—even just an hour or two spent together—can be a wonderful thing.

Give Gifts with Longevity and Purpose

Instead of the latest fad toy, consider giving gifts with a longer shelf life. Books are ideal because they can be passed on to a younger friend or donated to the local library when your child outgrows them. Art and craft supplies offer fun for playtime as well as inspiration for gifts.

Board games bring family and friends together. Sports equipment and music encourage movement and social time.

Forget Buying Gift Wrap (Unless You Really Love It)

Wrap your gifts in kid-generated art, newspaper, butcher paper, or plain brown paper. Decorate with yarn. Asha's family draws "ribbons" on the packages and adds funny gift labels such as "Freeze-dried lettuce" and "Lifetime supply of socks."

Be Charitable

Instilling the concept of charitable giving in kids will help them see the world beyond their own immediate surroundings.

Isabel Kallman of AlphaMom.com, via BostonMamas.com: Volunteer at food pantries with your family. Do your holiday shopping at sites such as iGive.com and iBakeSale.com that direct a percentage of their sales to charities of your choice. Donate credit card points and frequent flyer miles to support charitable organizations for those who can't afford to enjoy the holidays with their families.

Support Local

Online shopping is wonderfully convenient, but there's something special (and powerful) about supporting local businesses and artisans. Make it part of your holiday tradition to patronize local stores, whether by visiting neighborhood shops or buying locally made gifts via Etsy.com.

Consider Tasteful Secondhand Treasures and Regifting

Careful selection, a little personalization, and creative packaging can turn secondhand purchases and unused items you already own into beautiful gifts. High-end gifts become affordable when they're "pre-owned" (Christine's secondhand baby shower was a testament to this point; see chapter 4 for details). Plus, it's perfectly okay to run the idea by the recipient in advance.

One of my friends recently had a baby and I wanted to send her a care package. I knew she was into babywearing, and I had a fantastic baby carrier that Violet didn't really take to. So I sent her a quick e-mail asking whether a gently used baby carrier would be appreciated and the answer was a resounding YES.

Use Gift-y Occasions as Opportunities to Declutter

We all love presents, but unless you adhere to the "one-in-one-out" rule, the inevitable (if gradual) result is clutter. Use birthdays and holidays (and any other occasion that produces an inflow of gifts) as reminders to edit your stuff.

Help Your Kids "Make Room" by Donating Old Toys

Kids' generous natures often get a boost when they know presents are on the way. Birthdays and holidays are natural opportunities to go through old toys with your child to "make room" *and* to donate to other kids.

Susan via Parent Hacks: I told my daughter that on Christmas Eve, when Santa comes to visit, he'll leave her new toys, but he'll also take old toys back with him so the elves can fix them up and send them to little boys and girls who may not get anything for Christmas.

She was all gung ho to collect her used toys for Santa, even including some of her favorites and telling us that the kids who don't have as many toys will love them even more than she does. On December 26, the box of toys will go in Grandma's trunk for a trip to the local women's shelter.

If You Can Manage It, Donate Rather Than Return Unwanted Gifts

If you find yourself with gifts you appreciate but don't truly want, follow this great tip from a *Parent Hacks* community member: skip time-consuming return lines and donate the items instead.

Meet the World: Vacation & Travel

Fun family travel. An oxymoron? We think not. While no one relishes the prospect of hours trapped on a plane with a screaming baby, that's not the stereotype we think family travel deserves. Travel is one of the best ways to introduce your child to the world living and breathing outside the bubble of his experience. Even a single vacation offers the chance to renew and deepen family relationships, learn something new, and have fun at the same time.

What's more, by exposing your kids to the wider world, you're helping build future citizens. Traveling while the kids are young inserts a global perspective into their DNA that continues to influence them long after they return home. Here we share our thoughts about fitting travel into a minimalized family life, as well as our strategies for reducing vacation hassle while increasing the potential for happy memories.

Challenge Your Budget and Availability

Are you *really* unable to take a couple days off to turn a weekend into a getaway? Are there expenses you can cut so you can funnel more cash into your travel budget? Push past the usual reasons of being too busy or it costing too much. Delegate work to colleagues, let some work wait for a few more days, or pack lunch for a month to make up for the money "lost" by forgoing another workday. In chapter 6 we talked about identifying the difference between an expense and an investment. If travel is a priority for your family, it's worth the investment.

 I'm fortunate to have a flexible schedule, and we cut corners money-wise and take the kids out of school to be able to afford the cost of travel. But some of our happiest vacation memories don't involve exotic destinations or fancy accommodations—just warm days playing in the pool at my cousin's house. All for the price of gasoline to drive there.

Rethink Big Travel

Sometimes making a vacation affordable simply requires reframing what constitutes a vacation in the first place. Travel doesn't have to be prohibitively expensive and sometimes it's less about the destination than it is about the time to be together.

 When I was a kid, air travel was financially impossible for our family of nine and time off from my parents' store was scarce. However, there were a couple of years when we all went to Cape Cod for a weekend. We'd pile into the big two-tone green van, busting with excitement over the prospect of time together that was free of household and store demands. I have vivid memories from those trips—I had never before seen my parents so at ease. These trips were never fancy, but we were all so happy and present in the moment.

Jon and I are fortunate to be able to take vacations with the girls. We're not extravagant but we typically take a few trips each year—whether they are weekend car trips to the Cape or Maine, or bigger trips requiring air travel. But to be honest, I don't really care where we go. It's less about the destination or itinerary; I just want the time and space to be present with my family.

If leaving home just isn't an option, there are plenty of ways to enjoy what's right around the corner. For example:

- **Get to know your neighborhood.** Visit the new ice cream parlor in the neighborhood. What's playing at the second-run movie theater? Check out your town's local event listings and take advantage of the fun your area has to offer.
- **Get active.** Get on your bikes, or go for a walk or hike. Assuming your kids are mobile, nothing ups an outing's fun quotient like getting out of the car.
- **Consider a local hotel.** If you need a change of scenery and can afford a short hotel stay, consider a night or two at a local hotel that you've always admired from the curb. Check around for

hotels with family-friendly programming: many larger hotels offer kids' club programs and activities.

Prepping & Packing

You know where you're going; your next job is to pack and get your family there. Here are some minimalist travel tips that will help you with your preparation.

Prep Your Destination

Save packing space (and your weary arms) by renting or borrowing items in advance of your trip (e.g., use the hotel crib). Opt for lodging with a kitchenette or at least a refrigerator so you can store perishables and save money by eating in for some of your meals. A suite or adjoining rooms means you don't have to sneak around in the dark once your kids go to bed.

Pack Wisely

A few simple tricks are all you need to lighten your load and get you on your way.

- **Limit your bags.** The less space you have, the less space you will fill. If possible, aim to travel with one piece of luggage and one carry-on, keeping in mind that you only have so many arms and may have other gear (e.g., stroller) to negotiate (also, remember that school-age kids can handle their own bags). *Boston Mamas* reader Chris, of sturdyblog.blogspot.com, recommends onebag.com for tips on how to pack light.
- **Think old school.** Bring the bare essentials (e.g., a compact stroller) and skip nonessentials (e.g., bouncy chair, lots of toys) that your parents' generation never bothered with. Your kids will no doubt find plenty of to keep themselves busy in their new surroundings.
- **Pack mix and match basics.** Get the most out of your wardrobe by packing items that you can wear repeatedly and simply refashion with space-saving accessories.
- **Stack and pack.** To save space, place all of your like-category clothing (e.g., shirts, pants) in a stack then fold over in half.

Folding clothes in a stack rather than individually saves room and also helps prevent wrinkling.

- **Do laundry at your destination.** Bring fewer clothes and run a load of laundry while on your trip. It may seem like a bummer to do laundry while on vacation but it means you'll have less to unpack and wash when you get home!
- **Be prepared.** Pack an extra outfit for your child and a backup T-shirt for yourself in your carry-on (because you know that if you don't, accidents will happen). Also, pack snacks. Always pack snacks!

Being Present

You've planned and packed and you're on vacation! Congratulations! We couldn't be happier for you. Now, kick your feet up and enjoy the moment.

- **Unplug.** The video games may have helped get you through the travel time, but now that you're at your destination, stow the electronic devices (except for the camera). That goes for the kids *and* the grown-ups. When the inevitable in-between moments are filled with video games and smartphone checks, chances to connect with each other and with the surroundings get lost. When Asha and her husband instituted this travel rule, at first there was protest, but even the kids now agree that vacations are more fun without the electronics.
- **Avoid overscheduling vacation time.** Set your expectations about seeing everything there is to see at your destination. Make a list of the top attractions you'd like to visit, then proceed as it feels good for everyone. Know that you can always come back another time to see more.

 When Jon and I first visited the United Kingdom, we opted for a "wake up and see what we feel like doing" approach to sightseeing that we have carried forward ever since. Every morning, we'd flip through the guidebook and decide what we wanted to do that day depending on our energy level and interests. It was *so* delightful to not have a structured itinerary, and we now take the same approach when we travel as a family (Laurel loves contributing input to the decisions!). Travel is supposed to be about doing what feels fun and interesting, not about slavishly checking must-see items off a list.

- **Don't sweat the sleeping schedule.** In general, it's good to keep kids on a relatively consistent schedule. But when you're traveling, go easy on yourself, especially if everyone's contending with jet lag. Kids often have a harder time napping in unfamiliar places, so they might skip their regular naps, or nap in the car or stroller, or end up going to bed early. You can't control all of the scheduling elements during travel, so spare yourself the stress.
- **Be open to new experiences.** Travel opens you and your kids up in ways that aren't possible when surrounded by the routines and trappings of home. You have an opportunity to discover new passions, break old habits, and find out things about your family you might never have known otherwise.

 On a recent trip to Hawaii, we tried SNUBA with our kids (a snorkeling/SCUBA diving combination that allows total beginners to swim underwater while breathing from an oxygen tank). It was a stretch— that is, we were risking a kid freak-out because of the physical challenge involved—but when Sam came back to the surface he was sputtering with excitement. "This is my new hobby! Who needs video games?" While his plans might not be realistic, his passion was real. He's now looking into getting certified for SCUBA diving.

When it comes to special occasions, holidays, and travel it really is possible to have your cake and eat it too. Stay focused on doing what brings you joy—you'll be amazed to find that the company and trimmings and surroundings will sparkle all the more.

14

YOU, Minimalist You!

There's a reason that this is the last chapter of *Minimalist Parenting*. Too often, last is exactly where you fall on the priority list (if you don't fall off the list altogether). But our intention is this: self-care should be the last thing you remember when you close this book...because you come *first* in your life.

We've all heard the tired metaphor about "putting your own oxygen mask on first." In theory, it makes sense. But carving out time for yourself, and, more importantly, internalizing that you *have a right* to that time, is easier said than done. Not only are there real constraints on your time, money, and mental capacity, there are real cultural associations between motherhood and martyrdom. To pretend we're immune to those pressures just isn't realistic.

When you become a parent your priorities naturally shift. But that doesn't mean you should disappear. We're not suggesting a return to the carefree days of yore or the crazy nights at the club. You're a different, multifaceted person now that you're a parent, and you need time to get to know—and celebrate—this new, glorious incarnation of YOU.

Self-Care Is Not Selfish

When you treat yourself well, goodness trickles down into your relationships with your partner, your kids, your friends, and your community. It's like a big circle of awesomeness.

What You Do Impacts Others

Your ability to take care of others is directly proportional to your own vitality and happiness. It's not that a pedicure will make you a better mother. It's that a happy, nourished person has more to give everyone.

Your Children Are Watching

Children see and hear everything. It's almost freaky how tuned in they are to our states of being. They know when you're depleted and will act (and react) accordingly. Some kids will dial up the drama in order to stay at the center of your attention, while others will scale back their needs and step into the caretaker role themselves. It's good for kids to see their parents as rounded, fallible individuals (not paragons of perfection), but it's also important that they trust you've got the basics handled so they can focus on their own growth. Self-care sets a crucial example for your kids about the relationship between taking care of yourself and being able to take care of others.

You've Already Created the Space!

At the very beginning of this book we talked about the concept of permission—that it's time to let yourself step off the overparenting treadmill to find the unique prescription that works for your family. You're on your way to minimizing physical and emotional clutter. You've created space in your life (or you will once you put this book down!) and it's time to give yourself the permission to make yourself a priority. Self-care is *not* indulgent or selfish—it is a crucial part of living a full life.

Putting Yourself Back on the Priority List

Much as we'd love to kick this chapter off with "WEEK AT THE SPA FOR EVERYONE!" that's not exactly realistic. Neither is suddenly spending five days a week at the gym, dropping $200 at the cosmetics counter, or meditating for an hour every night. We prefer to think of self-care as a habit and an attitude to develop more than as something to simply "do."

When you're juggling home and work demands, it can feel impossible to find time for yourself. We totally get it. We've been there. Possibly even yesterday. Try these strategies as you ease yourself into new "you" parameters:

Start Small

It's tempting to set big self-care goals, but you're more likely to succeed if you start small. Christine once read in a running magazine that ten minutes of running is better than no running. That concept resonated because really, don't we all deserve at least ten minutes a day to focus on ourselves? Without a doubt. Set your sights on carving out ten minutes a day for yourself and build from there.

Schedule Self-Care in Your Calendar

This tip is particularly suited to those who live by their to-do lists and calendars (which we hope you're doing after listening to our productivity evangelizing in chapter 2). Put self-care on your recurring daily to-do list (read on for ideas about what your self-care might entail). You'll feel really happy every day when you check it off.

Focus on the Present

In the beginning, self-care can be difficult to enjoy because it's hard to ignore the work and household matters looming in the background. Try to notice how much calmer you feel when you focus on one thing at a time. When you're present in the moment, you can bring all of your energy and creativity to whatever you're doing at the time, including doing something good for yourself. So when you've got your ten minutes (or more!) set aside, shut off everything else and just focus on yourself.

Ask for Help

When you let go of the need to manage every detail, you open up the opportunity to ask for help. Do it! Asking for help is *not* a weakness. It does not mean that you are incapable of doing something—it simply means you are opting not to do something at that moment. Embrace that other people may get to the finish line in a totally different way than you would, and go with it.

Say No

Hopefully, chapter 3 convinced you that it's okay (more than okay!) to say no to things you don't want to do. We're reminding you again, because it's easy to fall into the trap of feeling selfish when you prioritize, say, your workout time over, say, a request to volunteer for a school field trip. You have the authority to make case-by-case decisions about how you use your time—don't simply default to neglecting yourself.

You get to define "self-care." As you customize your approach to your new minimalist life, keep in mind that you are driving the bus. Make joy a goal. You deserve happiness. Every day.

Fitness: Finding Your Strength One Step at a Time

Yeah, yeah. Exercise. Good for the body and the soul. Part of a reasonable weight-management strategy. Important component of cardiovascular fitness. Healthy people do it. The government wants you to do it. You know you should do it.

When did fitness become associated with *should*? We like this reasoning better: it's fun, it's easy to integrate into your life, and it will boost your self-confidence and reveal your strength in ways nothing else will. Your goal needn't be Olympic athlete, marathon runner, cover model, or fifteen pounds of lost weight. You just need to move. That's it. Walk, dance, run, bike, swim, hike…whatever makes you feel good.

The beauty of fitness is that starting *anywhere fun* leads to momentum in the right direction. We know that the newspaper reports and health experts talk about exercising X number of minutes for Y number of days per week. But you also know what we think about experts— they're helpful, but they're not living your life. *You* decide where and how to begin. Here are some simple ways to get on, stay on, or climb back on the fitness wagon.

Ten to Fifteen Minutes Is Still Worth It

Pursuant to the "think small" point earlier, remember that any bit of effort is great. Don't be hindered by the idea that if you can't do a full forty-five minute workout it isn't worth it.

Set Small, Achievable Goals

If goal setting helps motivate you to prioritize yourself, do it, but start small. It's great to think about larger, long-term goals, but they can be daunting when you're getting back to fitness. Instead, set smaller goals such as "Run ten minutes" or "Do five push-ups" (apps such as Couch to 5K are great for novice runners who need help setting small concrete goals). You get to decide what "starting small" looks like for you.

Get Inspired by Social Media

Use social media both for inspiration and to support other friends who are trying to carve out self-care time. There's something oddly motivating about sharing that you're waffling about a run and then having a bunch of people tweet or Facebook you, barking at you to get your butt out the door.

Build Fitness Into Everyday Activities

Sometimes the best way to fit in exercise is to literally speed up your everyday activities. This doesn't jibe with our ideal recommendation to focus on one thing at a time, but sometimes it's what works.

 During the weekdays—in which I have limited child care but a full workload—the best way for me to get in my fitness is to build it in to what I'm already doing. I walk Violet to day care to warm up and then run home. Or I run to and from errands. I've even run to and from business meetings (fortunately, my colleague Morra doesn't mind when I show up sweaty for brainstorming sessions).

I once wrote a tongue-in-cheek *Parent Hacks* blog post called "The Crazy Parent Workout!!!" In it, I described how, when grocery shopping with my then-preschooler, I'd park on the far side of the lot, plop her into a cart, and then run to the store entrance. To the rest of the world, I probably looked insane, but my daughter loved the high-speed cart rides, I got my heart pumping, and my errands were finished in record time.

Exercise with Friends

Meet up with friends for a run, walk, or fitness class. Sign up for a race together. Other people will help hold you accountable and you'll have the lovely benefit of grown-up social time (another critical component of self-care).

Log Your Accomplishments

If you dig data collection, sign up with a service like DailyMile.com. You can share workouts, get mileage reports, and connect with people to motivate and congratulate one another. Christine is also a fan of the MyFitnessPal app for tracking workouts, and as a way to be more mindful about what she's eating.

Gear Up

If your yoga gear is ill-fitting or threadbare you won't feel comfortable downward dogging. Cuteness counts, too. Spring for some good-quality gear so you can get moving safely and comfortably.

Change Up Your Routine

Getting bored? Ride your bike instead of walking. Take a Zumba class instead of step aerobics. Ignore the intimidation and go for it. You're stronger than you realize.

Sign Up and Stick with It

Sometimes a class is a good motivator. Via *Boston Mamas*, Heather of RookieMoms.com recommends, "Pay for a class so you make it a priority." And Jennifer of HeyGirlMommaGo.com recommends that you prioritize your own "enrichment" classes just as you would for your kids: "I take a BodyJam dance class that I adore and I treat it like I would my son's karate class or my daughter's ballet...I don't miss it!"

Do Whatever Works

Try putting on your workout clothes first thing in the morning and stink yourself out. (Gross? Maybe, but it works.)

One surprisingly effective way to get myself to exercise is to put on my workout clothes first thing in the morning and not allow myself to shower until I have done something. *Anything.* I recently had a day where I was planning on a run but it kept getting pushed off for one reason or another. Finally, even though I usually don't run in the late afternoon, I couldn't take my stinky self anymore and hit the pavement for a quick ten-minute run. The shower felt even more delicious afterward.

Style: Small Tweaks Go a Long Way

Your "style" is, by definition, personal. Just as you're defining your own unique parenting path, you—not *Vogue* or department store clothing buyers—get to decide which style works for you.

Style is an important aspect of self-care, even if you don't consider yourself a fashionista. We all like to feel pretty, put together, or at least *clean*. Wherever your style baseline is, small tweaks can do wonders for your self-image, and you don't need to invest a lot of time. Here are a few pointers to get you started.

Don't Feel Bad About Wanting to Look Good

This is an important point to start with. Women are pelted with the conflicting messages that it's shallow to focus on your looks AND that you should aspire to the images in the magazines. Confusing as this may be, the good news is that neither message is true—you can still be smart and competent and want to look put together...but you don't have to follow the lead of the fashion press.

Declutter Your Closet and Cosmetics Drawer

The decluttering methods we discussed in chapter 5 apply to your closet and cosmetics drawer as well.

 For a long time my closet was replete with "hopefuls." Things I hoped would fit again someday. Things I hoped would come back into style. Things I regretted buying but hoped I would stop regretting someday. The idea of doing a complete closet overhaul (where you take everything out, sort it, then only put back the true keepers) overwhelmed me, so I decided to take a more gradual approach: whenever I got dressed in the morning, any hopefuls that I pulled out as possibilities but didn't choose to wear, I put into the donation bag. Over the course of a couple of weeks I effectively trimmed the contents of my closet until it was full of clothes I felt happy wearing.

Figure Out Your Most Flattering Styles

You already know this, but the clothes that look good on a six-foot, size-zero model will not necessarily look good on you. But damn, it's tempting to try. It may take some trial and error (save your receipts!), but try to take note of which silhouettes are most comfortable and flattering. Run with those as your closet workhorses. This isn't to say that you shouldn't experiment with other styles, but it's good to build a closet of go-to wardrobe options and then explore from there as your budget allows.

Be Okay with Gradual Style Acquisition

People vary in how confident they feel about their style. Perhaps you're still searching. Flip through magazines and flag looks your eye naturally gravitates toward, go shopping with a style-savvy friend, or shop at a department store that offers free personal consultations to help you think differently about your wardrobe.

Get out of the Yoga Pants . . . at Least a Few Times a Week

If you're not dressing for work or a specific occasion, it is *very* tempting to pull on the yoga pants and wear them for the next forty-eight hours. We get it. But think how good it will feel to take ten minutes (seriously, that is all it takes) to focus on you. Pull on a skirt or pair of pants, a cute top, and a pretty necklace. Done. Christine's also a big fan of dresses as no-brainer wardrobe staples. Pair with earrings or a necklace, a pair of sandals or flats, and a cute belt or bag and you're dressed in minutes.

Identify the Gaps in Your Wardrobe and Acquire Accordingly

Once you have identified what you enjoy wearing and what will get a lot of wear, make a list of what you need. Keep it somewhere handy (your to-do list!) so when a good sale pops up at your favorite store, you can grab the essentials.

Befriend Accessories

Unwilling to commit to bold color and pattern in your wardrobe staples? It's time to befriend accessories.

Though I love fashion, I don't like to invest in a lot of prints or pieces that are, well, easily identifiable. My tendency is to shop for mix and match neutrals and then use accessories to add color and finish the look. In particular, I love statement necklaces and adding pops of color via bags, shoes, or belts. I'm also a major fan of red lipstick.

Take Time for Basic Grooming

It's a cliché of modern motherhood that one doesn't have time for a shower. It's not true. You're worth the ten minutes it takes to shower and run a comb through your hair, even if it's during the delirious moments before you fall into bed.

Schedule Appointments Ahead of Time

If you're in dire need of a haircut, schedule one *right now*, even if you can only get an appointment three weeks from now. It will be sitting there on your calendar and you'll be able to work it into your schedule. When you're at the salon paying for your haircut and the receptionist asks if you'd like to schedule a follow-up appointment, say YES, and book it right then and there. While we're talking about appointments, same goes for doctor and dentist visits. Address health issues while they are small so they don't grow into larger and more expensive problems.

MINIMALIST BEAUTY

We love Sarah James of Whoorl.com for her down-to-earth approach to beauty. We asked her to share her favorite doable beauty solutions.

Think of Your Skin

I've been known to stare at my little ones' perfectly smooth skin and pine for the good ol' days. Truth of the matter is that as we approach our late thirties and forties, things definitely start to change with regard to our skin. Fine lines and wrinkles, hyperpigmentation, uneven tone…well, it's not the most fun. However, don't let the myriad skin care options scare you away. Skin care doesn't have to be intimidating or time consuming! Stick to a one, two, three punch: cleanse, treat, moisturize. Cleanse with a gentle cleanser, treat any skin concern you might have with a serum and/or exfoliant, and moisturize.

How do you wade through the plethora of skin care options? Talk to your friends, read reviews online, grab skin care samples when you're out and about…find what works for you. However, I personally feel that skin looks its best when you keep your routine simple and focus on living well. Like Audrey Hepburn said, "I believe that happy girls are the prettiest."

The Five-Minute, Five-Product Face

As much as I like to experiment with new looks, I'm usually applying makeup with one foot out the door. It's wonderful to have a beauty "game face," meaning a tried and true, effortless look that makes you feel ready for the world. Five beauty essentials for moms on the go are concealer, an eyelash curler, mascara, cream blush, and lip gloss. These five products are perfect for enhancing your own natural beauty, as well as disguising the fact that you got three hours of sleep last night.

Low-Maintenance Hair

For moms, the key to lovely, manageable hair is a low-maintenance style. I mean, truly, who has a huge chunk of time to spend on her hair in the morning? (Not me!) If you have gorgeous cheekbones, why not go for a chic pixie? If short hair isn't your cup of tea, the easiest styles to manage are shoulder length and longer. Long layers give hair movement, and longer styles open the door to all sorts of updos, such as topknots and smooth ponytails, giving you ample ways to style your hair in a hurry. My hair secret? I wash my hair in the evening, wrap it in a loose bun while damp, go to bed, and voilá, instantly smooth and shiny waves the next morning when I release the bun. Total time saver.

Relaxation: Let's Do This Thing

We tend to forget that time and space to relax is an important aspect of self-care. It can be a ten-minute window during which you flip through a magazine, go for a walk, knit, or sip a cup of tea and do absolutely nothing. If you have more time, try a little pampering, chatting with a good friend, a movie, doing something creative, sleeping, or experimenting with new hobbies.

Allyson via the Minimalist Parenting blog: I still make "grown-up" meals. We eat a wide variety of foods that are tasty and good for us. It helps that our toddler has somewhat gourmet tastes ("I dinosaur! Dinosaurs eat SALMON!"), but preparing and eating good food still feels like a self-care treat, even when you're cleaning bits of it off the floor/your hair/your spouse's shirt.

 Ingrid via the Minimalist Parenting blog: When my daughter was small, bedtime was difficult because if I was around, she wouldn't settle down unless I was with her, so I would go out to the library one or two nights a week, leaving her and her father to develop their own routine. I would read and sometimes knit, often browse through magazines, or take my laptop and surf the web…sometimes I would go window-shopping with a latte in hand. My girl is older now and manages bedtime very well, but I still love the occasional evening at the library.

Minimalist Parenting ultimately makes room for you to experience life more fully. To quiet your mind. Relax your body. Breathe deeply. Eat mindfully. Be present. Each time you find yourself with free time, grab it with joyful hands.

You and Your Partner

One of the many benefits of taking care of yourself is the natural brightening effect it has on your relationship with your partner. Your growing ease and self-confidence will help you loosen your grip on simmering resentment, and opens the door to productive conversation. Bonus: your uptick of attention to your appearance might garner some appreciative glances as well.

But we all know how rough parenting can be on a partnership, and you—like most of us—could probably use some bolstering in the romance department. Part of caring for yourself includes nurturing your relationship—both fixing the stuff that's broken and encouraging the stuff that brought you together in the first place.

Avoid Festering

People differ in how they express their emotions—some let it all hang out, others clamp down on their emotions. Declare an open communication pact with your partner; you can more quickly diffuse tense situations and clear up misunderstandings when you talk things out instead of keeping quiet. Think of all the energy you will save for better things!

If You Can't Work It Out, Get Help

Sometimes it's hard to see your way through relationship issues when you're right in the middle of them. Working with a therapist is not a sign of a weak relationship; it's actually a sign of strength that you're willing to invest time and energy in your partnership. Having someone else in the room, even for a few sessions, can help everyone feel heard so you can clear out old resentments and make room for a new story that feeds you both.

Take Your Own Baggage Elsewhere

Parents often have little time to catch up and enjoy each other as couples. When Christine struggles with issues that don't relate to the family, she'll often seek out the help of a friend or therapist instead of clogging her time with Jon.

Trust and Be Supportive

You and your partner might not agree on the specifics of how to solve a problem (be it personal, professional, or related to parenting). But as long as you're on the same page about the result, support and trust in each others' competence and good intention.

Prioritize "We" Time

For a relationship to survive (and thrive!), you need to get out and actually talk and listen to one another, away from the clamor of family life. Put date night on the calendar, even if it's only once a month. Try to get away together from time to time, even if it's just one night. If baby-sitting is prohibitively expensive, consider swapping babysitting time with friends or calling on help from family.

 Tiffany via the Minimalist Parenting blog: We have made it a point to travel together when child care is available. We do a lot together as a family, but my husband and I find traveling together is just as important (whether it's a night away or two weeks away). Our being gone also helps the kids develop flexibility and independence, and shows them that their mom and dad love each other and enjoy spending time together.

Make More Time for Pointless Fun

When you're a parent, it's too easy to let your relationship turn into a management partnership—all logistics, no fun. Swap some of the household to-dos for some goof-off time together.

Small Acts of Kindness Have a Big Impact

Sometimes the smallest acts garner the most attention. Christine is convinced that her coffee tastes much better when Jon makes it for her. And those small acts remind her to reciprocate, too.

Ask for Help and Respond to Requests Directly and Respectfully

It can be hard to ask for help and also hard to say no. Agree that each party is allowed to ask the other for help *and* that the other person has permission to say yes or no, trusting that both parties are operating from a baseline of helpfulness and support.

Allow Each Other Time for Mindfulness

As we hurry through life, there's such comfort and value in encouraging each other to slow down and take more time, whether it's while doing errands or when slipping off to a café for some solo time.

Respect the Roles You Each Play

Whether both of you work outside the home or one person is at home with the kids while the other works, both roles are important and warrant respect. *Boston Mamas* contributor Priya (a sixty-plus-hours-per-week attorney whose husband stays at home with their two kids) recommends these three elements as essential to developing a baseline of respect:

- **Resist correcting each other's parenting.** Constant correction can foster a sense of insecurity and resentment in the parent being corrected.
- **Hear each other out.** Both parties deserve time to vent a little—just because one parent got to spend the day in casual clothes at the park doesn't necessarily mean the day was easy.
- **Share the "firsts."** If one parent experiences a child's milestone first, allow the other parent the time and space to experience it with joy, instead of feeling guilty or resentful about missing out.

You and Your Wider Social Circle

Finally, there's the community beyond your family. You've got friends and family who nurture you in unique ways. However you choose to connect and in whatever setting (one on one, small group), reserve time to deepen and enjoy your friendships and your relationships with extended family. Explore how community involvement might enrich your life. By nurturing your wider social circle, you are ultimately building a support system that will make parenting richer and more fun.

Amid all your roles—parent among them—you're still *you*. Glorious you. Minimalist Parenting gives you the time and space to explore who you are now, and who you have yet to become.

Afterword: What's Next

We applaud you. Seriously. It's hard work to challenge your assumptions and priorities, and to open your mind to a new way of thinking. We are so grateful that you've trusted us on this journey. *You've invested in yourself and your family.*

We hope that *Minimalist Parenting* has equipped you with the inspiration and pragmatics to craft a family life that is uniquely and happily yours. There's no rush to the finish line (in fact, there is no finish line); take the time and however many big or baby steps you need to follow your newly-cleared path.

So what's next?

We want to continue the dialog! Visit the *Minimalist Parenting* website (minimalistparenting.com) for more ideas, printable resources, active challenges, and other inspiration. We're also on Twitter at @bostonmamas and @parenthacks and on Facebook at facebook.com/MinimalistParenting. Let's keep talking about the challenges and successes.

You're on your way to remarkable. GO YOU.

Resources

Throughout *Minimalist Parenting* we've mentioned a number of resources and have even more to share here. We hope this list helps you continue on your minimalizing journey! (For clickable links to all of these resources and more, visit MinimalistParenting.com.)

Parenting

Books

Faber, Adele, and Elaine Mazlish. *How To Talk So Kids Will Listen & Listen So Kids Will Talk.* New York: Scribner, 2012. (Fantastic model for respectful communication with kids)

Hoefle, Vicki. *Duct Tape Parenting: A Less Is More Approach to Raising Respectful, Responsible, and Resilient Kids.* Boston: Bibliomotion, 2012. (Practical advice to let kids learn from life)

Kohn, Alfie. *Unconditional Parenting: Moving from Rewards and Punishments to Love and Reason.* New York: Atria Books, 2006. (Recommended by Christine's husband, Jon)

Levine, Madeline. *The Price of Privilege: How Parental Pressure and Material Advantage Are Creating a Generation of Disconnected and Unhappy Kids.* New York: Harper, 2006. (Commentary on the "more is more" parenting climate)

Levine, Madeline. *Teach Your Children Well: Parenting for Authentic Success.* New York: Harper, 2012. (Authentic, values-based parenting)

Mogel, Wendy. *The Blessing of a Skinned Knee: Using Jewish Teachings to Raise Self-Reliant Children.* New York: Scribner, 2008. (Great read no matter what your religious background)

Payne, Kim John, and Lisa Ross. *Simplicity Parenting: Using the Extraordinary Power of Less to Raise Calmer, Happier, More Secure Kids.* New York: Ballantine, 2010. (The title says it all)

Skenazy, Lenore. *Free-Range Kids: How to Raise Safe, Self-Reliant Children (Without Going Nuts with Worry).* Hoboken: Jossey-Bass, 2010. (Landmark book addressing the overparenting phenomenon)

Websites

AlphaMom.com (Smart talk on parenting)
AskMoxie.com (Thoughtful, insightful parenting discussion)
LoveThatMax.com ("A blog about kids with special needs who kick butt")
ManicMommies.com (Website and weekly podcast for working parents)
Pbs.org/parents (Trusted source of conversation)
SimpleMom.net (Fantastic perspective on simple family living)
TheHappiestMom.com (Happier lives, one day at a time)
TheMotherhood.com (Community + live chats on a range of topics related to parenting)
Wired.com/geekdad (Enthusiastic, geeky dads share their passions)

Children's Behavior/Development

Books

Carter, Christine. *Raising Happiness: 10 Simple Steps for More Joyful Kids and Happier Parents.* New York: Ballantine, 2010. (Science and storytelling about raising happy kids)

Coloroso, Barbara, *The Bully, the Bullied, and the Bystander: From Preschool to High School--How Parents and Teachers Can Help Break the Cycle.* New York: William Morrow, 2009. (Our community recommends this book)

Galinsky, Ellen. *Mind In the Making: The Seven Essential Life Skills Every Child Needs.* New York: William Morrow, 2010. (A must read)

Greene, Ross W. *The Explosive Child: A New Approach for Understanding and Parenting Easily Frustrated, Chronically Inflexible Children.* New York: Harper, 2010. (Excellent, practical reframing of the "difficult child" label)

Hallowell, Edward M. *The Childhood Roots of Adult Happiness: Five Steps to Help Kids Create and Sustain Lifelong Joy.* New York: Ballantine, 2003. (Dr. Hallowell deeply appreciates kids' individuality)

Harris, Robie H., and Michael Emberley. *It's Perfectly Normal: Changing Bodies, Growing Up, Sex, and Sexual Health.* Somerville: Candlewick Press, 2009.(It's better that the kids get their sex education from you)

Huebner, Dawn, and Bonnie Matthews. *What to Do When You Worry Too Much:*

A Kid's Guide to Overcoming Anxiety. Washington, DC: Magination Press, 2005. (An anxiety workbook for kids)

Kindlon, Dan, and Michael Thompson. *Raising Cain: Protecting the Emotional Life of Boys*. New York: Ballantine Books, 2000. (For parents of boys)

Manassis, Katharina. *Keys to Parenting Your Anxious Child*. Hauppauge: Barron's Educational Series, 2008. (Recommended by Christine's friend Phoebe, a clinical child psychologist)

Wiseman, Rosalind. *Queen Bees and Wannabes: Helping Your Daughter Survive Cliques, Gossip, Boyfriends, and the New Realities of Girl World*. New York: Three Rivers Press, 2009. (For parents of girls)

Time Management and Productivity

Books

Allen, David. *Getting Things Done: The Art of Stress-Free Productivity*. New York: Penguin Books, 2002. (Recommended by our community)

Covey, Stephen R., Merrill, A. Roger, and Merrill, Rebecca R. *First Things First*. New York: Simon & Schuster, 1996. (Values-based approach to time management)

Francis, Meagan. *The Happiest Mom: 10 Secrets to Enjoying Motherhood*. San Francisco: Weldon Owen, 2011. (So much more than a productivity book! Self care, organization, wise, warm humor…much more)

Websites

FlyLady.net (E-mail based service that helps you develop home routines—with a super-devoted following)

LifeHacker.com (Tips, tricks, and technology for living better in the digital age; recommended by our community)

MyTomatoes.com (Web-based productivity timer system)

ZenHabits.net (Finding simplicity amid the chaos of daily life)

Paper Calendars and Planners

Franklin Covey (The organizer that propelled Christine's productivity to new heights in college)

Get Buttoned Up (Well-designed productivity and storage tools)

MomAgenda (Day planner oriented toward mothers' schedules)

Moleskine (Asha's favorite notebook for doodling and journaling)

Online Calendars, Planners and Apps

Cozi (Calendar management)

Dropbox (File sharing so you can have your to-do list handy at all times)

Evernote (Virtual bulletin board)
Google Calendar (Free online calendar)
Orchestra (To-do lists and more)
Things for iPhone (Asha's favorite to-do list app)

Organization and Decluttering

Books

Leeds, Regina, and Francis, Meagan. *One Year to an Organized Life with Baby: From Pregnancy to Parenthood, the Week-by-Week Guide to Getting Ready for Baby and Keeping Your Family Organized.* Cambridge: Da Capo Lifelong, 2011. (Step-by-step organization)

Oxenrider, Tsh. *Organized Simplicity: The Clutter-Free Approach to Intentional Living.* Cincinnati: BetterWay, 2010. (Practical guide to simple living)

Oxenrider, Tsh. *One Bite at a Time: 52 Projects for Making Life Simpler.* 52bites.com. (Inspiring, action-oriented ebook)

Walsh, Peter. *It's All Too Much: An Easy Plan For Living A Richer Life With Less Stuff.* New York: Simon & Schuster, 2007. (Less stuff! We agree)

Websites

CatalogChoice.com (Reduce junk mail)
Craigslist.org (Buy, sell, list stuff for free)
DonationTown.org (Free donation pickup)
Ebay.com (Good for selling higher value items that are worth shipping)
Freecycle.org (Find free stuff, give away stuff for free)
Goodwill.org (Make a difference through donation)
MabelsLabels.com (Personalized labels for everything)
MomAdvice.com (Organizing, frugal living, and more)
PeaceLoveSwap.com (Swap events)
SwapMamas.com (Baby goods swap site)
TheSwapaholics.com (Swap events)
Zwaggle.com (Parent swap network)

Rentals/Outsourcing

Airbnb.com (Home rental)
Amazon.com (Bulk buying deals; many in our community recommend the Amazon Mom's Subscribe & Save diaper and wipe delivery service)
Care.com (Child care services, as well as help for adults/seniors, pets, home)
Diapers.com (Lightning-fast diaper delivery)
Drugstore.com (Save yourself another errand)
Merrymaids.com (Housecleaning services)

Netflix.com (Movie rental)
RenttheRunway.com (Cocktail dress rental)
Sittercity.com (Child care)
TaskRabbit.com (Errand services)
Yelp.com (Local services search engine/review platform)
Zipcar.com and Car2Go.com (Car sharing)

Money

Books

Clark, Amy Allen, and Murphy, Jana. *The Good Life for Less: Giving Your Family Great Meals, Good Times, and a Happy Home on a Budget.* New York: Penguin (Perigree), 2012. (Positive, practical, frugal tips)

Greenslate, Christopher, Kerri Leonard. *On a Dollar a Day.* New York: Hyperion, 2010. (Get inspired to eat for a lot less)

Quinn, Jane Bryant. *Making the Most of Your Money.* New York: Simon & Schuster, 2009. (It's thick but readable, and tells you everything you need to know about your entire financial picture; in fact, if you read this single book, you've got pretty much all you need to know)

Ramsey, Dave. *The Total Money Makeover.* Nashville: Thomas Nelson, 2009. (We haven't read it ourselves, but many of our community members rave about Dave Ramsey's work)

Tyson, Eric. *Personal Finance for Dummies.* Hoboken: For Dummies, 2012. (Surprisingly useful intro to the fundamentals)

Websites

BabyCheapskate.com (Save money on baby gear)
BudgetsAreSexy.com (Make budgeting fun…and apparently sexy!)
GetRichSlowly.org (Smart personal finance)
Napfa.org (National Association of Personal Financial Advisors; good place to find local referrals)
TheCentsibleLife.com (Where motherhood and money meet)
TheSimpleDollar.com (Practical money-saving advice)
Wisebread.com (Active community conversation about saving money)

Financial Tools

Adaptu.com (Financial tracking)
ImpulseSave.com (Savings tool)
KiddyBank (App for allowance tracking)
Mint.com (Financial tracking)
SmartyPig.com (Savings tool)

Play

Books

Buchanan, Andrea J., and Miriam Peskowitz. *The Daring Book for Girls*. New York: William Morrow, 2012. (Essential girlhood skills)

Flett, Heather Gibbs, and Whitney Moss. *The Rookie Mom's Handbook*. Philadelphia: Quirk Books, 2008. (Activities to do with and without your new baby)

Iggulden, Conn, and Iggulden, Hal. *The Dangerous Book for Boys*. New York: William Morrow, 2012. (Essential boyhood skills)

Jacobs, Meredith, and Jacobs, Sofie. *Just Between Us: A No-Stress, No-Rules Journal for Girls and their Moms*. San Francisco: Chronicle Books, 2010. (A wonderful way to inspire communication between mother and daughter; we hope they come out with a version for boys, or a general parent/child version!)

King, Bart. *The Big Book of Boy Stuff*. Layton: Gibbs Smith, 2004. (Fun playtime inspiration; pretty much anything by Bart King will spark kids' imaginations)

Websites

DesignMom.com (Creative ideas for kids and parents alike)

FamilyFun.go.com (Crafts, recipes, and other inspiration)

KidsCraftWeekly.com (Craft ideas for kids)

KidsGardening.org (Gardening resources)

LetsPlay.com (Inspiring families outdoors, building playgrounds across the country)

MakeandTakes.com (Craft ideas for kids)

Nwf.org/Kids.aspx (The National Wildlife Federation's resource hub to inspire outdoor exploration)

RookieMoms.com (Go-to destination if you're new on the parenting block)

Education and School

Llewellyn, Grace, and Silver, Amy. *Guerrilla Learning: How to Give Your Kids a Real Education with or without School*. Hoboken: Wiley, 2001. (Thought-provoking book about education and learning)

Penn, Audrey, Harper, Ruth E., and Leak, Nancy M. *The Kissing Hand*. Terre Haute: Tanglewood Press, 2007. (A children's book to help with the transition to school)

Websites

KhanAcademy.org (Mindblowing collection of online lectures)

Food

Books/Cookbooks

Bittman, Mark. *How to Cook Everything*. Hoboken: Wiley, 2008.(Easy, modern basic reference)

Goldfarb, Aviva. *The Six O'Clock Scramble*. New York: St. Martin's Griffin, 2006. (Asha's go-to weeknight cookbook by the founder of The Scramble.com)

Knight, Karin, and Ruggiero, Tina. *The Best Homemade Baby Food on the Planet*. Beverly: Fair Winds Press, 2010. (Cookbook for those who dig making baby food)

Madison, Deborah. *Vegetarian Cooking for Everyone*. New York: Clarkson Potter, 2007. (Recommended by a reader as a great resource for vegetarian recipes)

Oliver, Jamie. *Jamie's Food Revolution*. New York: Hyperion, 2011 (Simple food, well prepared, great guy)

Stern, Michelle. *The Whole Family Cookbook: Celebrate the Goodness of Locally Grown Foods*. Avon, Massachusetts: Adams Media, 2011. (Family-friendly meals with a local foods focus)

Waters, Alice. *The Art of Simple Food*. New York: Clarkson Potter, 2007. (One of the original simple food gourmets)

Websites/Apps

Dinewise.com (Prepared meal service)

FreshDirect.com (Grocery delivery – New York area)

GroceryIQ.com (Grocery list tool recommended by our community)

How to Cook Everything app (Fantastic functionality for a cookbook app)

Netgrocer.com (Grocery delivery)

Peapod.com (Grocery delivery)

Relish.com (Healthy recipe database)

ThePioneerWoman.com (Amazing recipes, photography, and storytelling)

TheScramble.com (Family-friendly menu planning service)

ThisWeekForDinner.com (Weekly menu inspiration)

WhatsCookingWithKids.com (Certified green mobile cooking school)

Celebrations and Special Occasions

Books

Seo, Danny, and Levy, Jennifer. *Simply Green Giving: Create Beautiful and Organic Wrappings, Tags, and Gifts from Everyday Materials*. New York: Collins, 2006. (Recommended by Melissa Massello of shoestringmag.com)

Seo, Danny. *Simply Green Parties: Simple and Resourceful Ideas for Throwing the Perfect Celebration, Event, or Get-Together.* New York: William Morrow, 2006.

Websites

BirthdayswithoutPressure.com. University of Minnesota Department of Family Social Science. (Resources for celebrating birthdays without all the baggage)

Etsy.com (If you're going to give a gift, try searching local and supporting indie)

Evite.com (Paperless invitation service)

HelenJane.com (Gracious, generous entertaining)

iGive.com (Shop for good, recommended by Isabel Kallman of AlphaMom.com)

PaperlessPost.com (Paperless invitation service)

ToysforTots.org (Donate to kids in need)

Travel

DeliciousBaby.com (Making travel with kids fun)

MotherofallTrips.com (Family travel tips and reflections)

OneBag.com (Tips for traveling light)

Packing Pro (List-making app recommended by our friends at CoolMomTech .com)

TravelsWithBaby.com (Guidebooks and tips)

WeJustGotBack.com (Family travel advice)

Lifestyle and Self-Care

Books/Magazines

Brown, Brené. *The Gifts of Imperfection: Let Go of Who You Think You're Supposed to Be and Embrace Who You Are.* Center City: Hazelden, 2010. (Wise advice about knowing yourself)

Chapman, C. C. *Amazing Things Will Happen: A Real World Guide on Achieving Success and Happiness.* Hoboken: Wiley, 2012 (All-around great person shares his most important lessons learned)

Clark, Tracey. *Elevate the Everyday.* Waltham: Focal Press, 2012. (Learn how to take awesome pictures)

McDowell, Dimity and Sarah Bowen Shea. *Run Like a Mother: How to Get Moving—and Not Lose Your Family, Job, or Sanity.* Kansas City: Andrews McMeel, 2012. (Down-to-earth running inspiration for parents)

Johnson, Whitney. *Dare, Dream, Do: Remarkable Things Happen When You Dare to Dream.* Boston: Bibliomotion, 2012. (How to find and follow your dreams)

Real Simple. (Lifestyle magazine including everyday simplicity tips and tricks)

Rubin, Gretchen. *The Happiness Project*. New York: Harper Perennial, 2011. (We all deserve happiness)

Rubin, Gretchen. *Happier at Home*. New York: Crown, 2012. (We especially deserve happiness at home)

Walrond, Karen. *The Beauty of Different*. Houston: Bright Sky Press, 2010. (Reminder that you're uncommonly beautiful)

Websites

CoolMomPicks.com (Shopping site with a happy focus on indie/mom-owned businesses)

DailyMile.com (Get social with your fitness tracking)

DesignForMinikind.com & DesignForMankind.com (Online curation of lovely things for kids and adults)

GoMighty.com (Inspiration to live a better life)

MyFitnessPal app (A food/fitness tracking app to help you become more mindful of calories going in and out)

PetitElefant.com (Lifestyle blog replete with easy DIY beauty recipes)

PostpartumProgress.com (Postpartum depression support and community)

SeeingTheEveryday.com (An online magazine about everyday wonders)

ShoestringMag.com (The best of budget living)

SimpleLovelyBlog.com (Truly simple and lovely picks)

Whoorl.com (Down to earth beauty and style)

WorkingCloset.com (Everyday, minimalist fashion)

Where to Find Christine and Asha

Other than at MinimalistParenting.com of course!

Christine Koh

ChristineKoh.com (About me)

BostonMamas.com (Parenting/lifestyle portal for families in Boston and beyond)

Also on Twitter (@bostonmamas), Facebook (facebook.com/bostonmamas), Pinterest (christinekoh), and Instagram (bostonmamas)

Asha Dornfest

AshaDornfest.com (About me)

ParentHacks.com (Forehead-smackingly smart parenting tips)

Also on Twitter (@parenthacks) and Facebook (facebook.com/parenthacks)

Acknowledgments

Christine Koh

As you may have gathered from reading this book, my childhood experiences embedded in my cells a longing for meaningful relationships—to be a valued, accepted part of a community. One gift that writing *Minimalist Parenting* has given me is a reminder that I am, in fact, blessed with many wonderful relationships.

Thank you to the BlissDom 2010 attendees who told me after my panel that I should write a book (I drafted the outline for *Minimalist Parenting* on the plane ride home and bought the domain name not long after). Thank you Whitney Johnson, for telling Bibliomotion they should talk to me, even though you didn't know I had a book idea, and Morra Aarons-Mele, for being a wonderful colleague and also the brilliant inspiration behind Pivot Boston (the stage on which the Bibliomotion connection took place). Gretchen Rubin, thank you for our early book conversations, and for guidance on agents once the *Minimalist Parenting* wheels were in motion.

Erika Heilman and Jill Friedlander at Bibliomotion—you have created an incredible new way of doing things that should be a model for all publishers. Our fellow Bibliomotion authors—you are a deep well of thoughtfulness, humor, and generosity. Josh Getzler—you are a trusted advisor and your feedback on the first draft of *Minimalist Parenting* was invaluable. Rusty Shelton, Barbara Henricks, Margaret Kingsbury, and your teams—thank you for your social media and marketing expertise and guidance.

Kristen Chase, Liz Gumbinner, Ellen Galinsky, Melissa Massello, Ellen Seidman, Aviva Goldfarb, Sarah James—thank you for sharing your wisdom despite having very full plates of your own. The countless parents who shared anecdotes via the Minimalist Parenting, Boston Mamas, and Parent Hacks communities—it was an honor to weave your stories into our manuscript. Karen Walrond—thank you for your counsel and brilliance in producing our book trailer and Jen Bolitho, Stephanie Brubaker, Leslie Fandrich, Sarah Hubbell, Jim Lin, Rachel Matthews, Irène Nam, Stephanie Precourt, and Maile Wilson, thank you for contributing the amazing photos that punctuated our script so beautifully.

To my brilliant coauthor Asha, I could write a whole book on what I learned in working with you. Thank you for joining me at Camp Mighty to talk about this dream, and agreeing to embark on this journey with me. Thank you for making this the most joyful entry into book writing possible. Thank you for knowing when to edit our to-do list and for picking up my to-do list items when I was coming apart at the seams. Thank you for your ever present support at so many levels.

To my dear friends and family—I can't list everyone but I love and appreciate you all so much. Rachel and James (in absentia) Koh, I'm not sure I'll ever be able to convey how much respect I have for what you experienced, parenting so many children under such challenging circumstances. George, Kyoungho, Jason, Jennifer, Stephanie, Sharon, thank you for being my teammates during those early years. Estelle, Marjorie, Christophe, Jonathan, Nancy, Led, Josh, Claudia, Peter, and Joanne—I truly couldn't ask for better in-laws. Patrick and Jeannie—thank you for so many laughs. Kate Fichter, Paige Lewin, Heidi Milne—thank you for helping me realize I could make a go of it with my creative leap. Nicola Majchrzak, Heather Hoffman, Heather Zuzenak—I value our dinners so much. Lynne and Kevin Lappin and Sharla and Frank Randazzo—thank you for all of the playdate swaps (several of which helped me meet book deadlines!). Anne Maka and Michael Dakin—we treasure your stateside visits so much. To my ONEMoms Ethiopia team—you all occupy a deep and special place in my heart. Mary—thank you for being the most incredible day care director in the history of the universe. Adelaide—thank you for all of your wise teachings.

And finally, Jon, Laurel, and Violet. Thank you for teaching me so much about myself and how to be a better person. Thank you for supporting my book journey; I know that I have shared many details of our lives and I hope that the result is what I intended: to convey the remarkable lessons I have learned from you all, with respect and deep gratitude. So many things in my life would not be possible—or would be completely meaningless—without you. I love you all.

Asha Dornfest

Ushering a book into the world resembles the long, remarkable process of parenthood, with all its surprises and opportunities for humility. Also: the deep knowledge that it's a group effort. I'll never be able to thank everyone that has contributed to my inspiration for *Minimalist Parenting*, but I'm grateful to you all.

My first and sloppiest mention goes to Christine, my multitalented co-author and dear friend. I'm so thankful for all you've taught me about partnership, work ethic, generosity, and friendship. Thank you for trusting me with your dream, and for giving me the space to make it my own.

I never would have met Christine were it not for the community that gave me a voice: my blog, Parent Hacks. I share credit for my part in this book with the thousands of parents and blogging colleagues who have sent in their tips, left comments, and participated in smart, generous conversation for the last seven years.

I echo Christine's thanks to everyone involved with the production of *Minimalist Parenting*: the inspiring moments made possible by the BlissDom and Camp Mighty events combined with Whitney Johnson's pixie dust; our amazing publishers, Erika, Jill and the rest of the Bibliomotion team; Josh Getzler of HSG Agency; Rusty Shelton of Shelton Interactive; Margaret Kingsbury and Jessica Krakoski of Cave Henricks; Karen Walrond of Chookooloonks for her video editing magic, and all the brilliant contributors to (and champions for) our book, blog, and video.

As we were writing *Minimalist Parenting*, Christine and I traveled to Ethiopia with the ONE Campaign. This experience placed our parenting assumptions into a global perspective for which I will always be grateful. Huge thanks to Ginny Wolfe and Jeannine Harvey of ONE for making such an experience possible. To the ONEMoms—Kelly Wickham, Liz Gumbinner, Maya Haile Samuelsson, Diana Prichard, Alice Currah, Rana DiOrio, Gabrielle Blair, Cathleen Falsani, Jennifer Howze, and Michelle Pannell—you gave the warmest embrace one could ask for. And to the people we met while in Ethiopia: you showed me we're all capable of great things.

My thanks to the educators in my kids' lives: Carol Hewig, Lisa O'Brien, Rick Short, Jennifer Edler, Kristin Werts, Melissa Dragich, Teri Geist, Cara Pettit, Abby Largo, and Charla Cunningham. The only way I could focus on a project of this scale was by knowing my kids were thriving in your care.

To my friends, neighbors and guides: so much of what's in this book came out of conversation with you. Alisa Mallinger, Judie Sedrick, Karen Einbinder, Kyran Pittman, Harriet Steinberg, Heather and Nate Angell, Mary Wells Pope, Lyla Wolfenstein, Mary Levy, Katrina Norwood, Jill Duval, and my beloved cousins, Leslee Koritzke and Hayley Alexander.

I want to express my heartfelt gratitude to my family, without whom none of this would exist. My wonderful parents, Rosalyn and Jagdish Jirge; parents in-law, Carol and Franklyn Dornfest; and brother and sister in-law, Robin and Eileen Dornfest.

To my children: you inspired everything I wrote here. Sam, your strength, humor, and perspective has added richness to my own. Mirabai, your wisdom and clarity astounds and delights me every single day. I love you both more than I can ever express, and I am so grateful to be your mother.

Finally, to my brilliant husband, Rael: thank you for supporting me through each step of our journey. Your light shines on everything I do.

Index

WHERE ELSE TO FIND CHRISTINE + ASHA

Christine can be found in a variety of places around the web. Her daily blog, Boston Mamas (bostonmamas.com; facebook.com/bostonmamas), is an award-winning lifestyle portal for parents in Boston and beyond; the site covers local finds, food, fashion, design, crafts, eco-living, fitness, family issues, and more. Christine started the site in 2006; shortly thereafter, she hung up her spurs as a music and brain scientist.

Christine also is a self-taught graphic designer whose work at Posh Peacock (poshpeacock.com) has been featured in *Brides*, Daily Candy, and *Pregnancy & Newborn*. She strategizes digitally at Women Online (wearewomenonline.com), advocates for social good at The Mission List (themissionlist.com), and helps women make their lives more awesome via Pivot Boston (pivotboston.com). She also enjoys eating, blogging, and running and works to inspire others to do the same via Eat. Blog. Run. (eatblogrun.com). She hopes to revive her personal blog Pop Discourse (popdiscourse.com) one of these days.

You can see Christine's full portfolio of work at christinekoh.com and follow along with her on Twitter (@bostonmamas), Pinterest (christinekoh), Instagram (bostonmamas), and YouTube (bostonmamas).

Asha spends most of her online time at Parent Hacks (parenthacks.com; facebook.com/parenthacks), a trusted source of "forehead-smackingly smart" parenting tips and advice since 2005. Described by readers as "life-changing" and "an island of civility in the parenting blogosphere," Parent Hacks has earned the three-time honor of being named "#1 Most Useful" of Babble's Top 50 Mom Blogs.

With the help of a smart, generous community of parents, Asha shares tips, workarounds and recommendations for making family life easier. Topics include organizing your home, managing your time, simplifying mealtime, school-year organization, travel with kids, fun projects, crafts, and activities and plenty more one-of-a-kind ideas.

Practical tips often open the door to great conversations, and some of the best tips appear in the comments, tweets and updates readers offer in response. Parent Hacks is a lively, illuminating place to hang out -- come on over!

Asha's busy with other projects as well. Keep tabs on what she's up to at AshaDornfest.com and follow along with her on Twitter (@parenthacks).